# Bedtime Thoughts for the Christian Mom

Devotionals to Challenge and Encourage
Mothers

Kimberly Wright

Trafford PUBLISHING®   www.trafford.com

North America & international
toll-free: 1 888 232 4444 (USA & Canada)
phone: 250 383 6864 ♦ fax: 812 355 4082

# DEDICATION

For my husband and best friend John. To think this all started just
because two people fell madly in love. You're my lobster.

# CONTENTS

# Acknowledgements

I want to first acknowledge my children, the very reason I have the privilege of being able to share this book. Justin, Seth, Cooper and Anabelle…I am so proud of you and to be your mother. God has great things in store for each one of you. I love you so much.

I want to appreciate the mothers in my life. First, my mother, Lynda, who has always been my biggest cheerleader and who taught me most about hard work and never giving up. My grandma, May Belle, whom I miss everyday and taught me most of what I know. My Aunt Jean who first planted the seed of Christ in my heart and loved me as her own. My mother-in-law, Dana, whose love and dedication to motherhood shaped the man I am blessed to spend my life with. I love you all.

Thank you so much to Margaret Traudt for editing this book for me. Without her expertise and words of encouragement along the way, I shudder to consider the outcome.

A special thank you to Susie Benda, my sweet friend, for allowing me to share part of her heart and email regarding motherhood. Susie is an amazing woman and mother and I am blessed to have her as part of my life.

Last but not least, thank you to American Mothers, Inc. for honoring me as the 2009 National Young Mother of the Year. I appreciate all AMI does to promote and honor motherhood, and it has been my privilege to represent such a remarkable organization.

# FOREWORD

Motherhood is the hardest yet most rewarding job we will ever have. Sometimes, the more insecurities we feel in our ability to raise healthy, happy children, the more we tend to think everyone else has *it all together*. We feel our only option is to fake it until we make it.

Kimberly's look at the heart of motherhood changes this by reminding us it is not what we do but the heart by which we do it. Kids are not Faberge eggs that are to be admired from afar and only handled for special occasions. Instead they are priceless works of art that provide us multiple opportunities to develop our character. Through her genuine ability to laugh at herself, Kimberly encourages all of us to love ourselves right where we are so God has a place to start.

Kimberly Malloy, BA MS
President, Train2excel, Inc.
Founder and Speaker, Starr Ministry

# PREFACE

My purpose for this booklet is two-fold. First, I love to read. Give me a book, a blanket, and a fireplace and I am in heaven. On the rare occasion my husband and I take a vacation alone, I will read four to six novels during our trip. On road trips we listen to books on tape so we can read while traveling.

But in day-to-day life with four active children, a dog, a home, and careers, reading is a luxury. Typically, I read booklets made for a short daily read. They are perfect for my nightstand and I can actually finish one in less than six months. I get my reading fix without feeling like I have one more thing on my to-do list I will never cross off. I wanted to write something in bite-size pieces for the busy mom like myself.

The second reason I wanted to write this is the more important. We mothers need each other. We need each other to help us grow personally and spiritually. We need someone to give words of encouragement and someone to share the highs and lows of motherhood.

I want to partner with you on this wonderful and unpredictable journey. As I said, I have four of my own little cherubs who daily test me, grow me, challenge me, frustrate me, anger me, surprise me, bless me and fill me with more love and passion than seems humanly possible. I am certain I love my children more than any other person has ever loved her children in the history of children. I am certain you feel the same way about yours.

With such fierce desire to be a great mother come feelings of failure and guilt on a too-often basis. *Did I spend enough time with this child? Why did I lose my temper over something so minor? Did it hurt his little feelings when I shooed him away while I was finishing the bills? Do I give the right help with homework? Are they getting enough fruits and vegetables? Will she be upset I can't go on the school field trip? Is it too harsh to make them do so many chores? Am I leading by the best example? Am I raising up a godly woman and godly men?* The doubts are endless.

So many nights I fall into bed exhausted, praying "Lord, I really blew it today. How can I be better tomorrow?" I lie there wondering, "Am I the only mother out there who can't keep up?" I feel like a tornado blowing through life out of control while everyone else seems to have it all together.

Don't you ever feel like you just need someone to whisper in your ear, "You are doing a good job"? Here are thirty-one bedtime stories – one for each day of the month – just for you, Mom.

It is my prayer you find encouragement and growth-provoking ideas which will challenge you. Each day has a scripture to meditate on and a challenge for you to put into practice. Hopefully this will give you a truth to ponder as you slip into your much-needed and much-deserved REM cycle. Thank you for sharing this journey with me.

Consider this your whisper, "Mom, you are doing a GREAT job."

# DAY ONE

## JESUS, THE SUN CAME UP

When my oldest son, Justin, was about three years old, he began getting out of his bed in the middle of the night and coming into ours. My husband and I had agreed we wanted our children to sleep in their own beds (as a general rule) and learn the independence of sleeping alone.

So I explained to Justin before bedtime, "Stay in your bed until the sun comes up. When you see the sun come up, you can come to our bed to cuddle with us." The "sun coming up" was the cue and what we referred to often. He grasped this idea.

One morning I got up before dusk and I went to the recliner in the living room with my Bible. It was quiet and peaceful as the sun began to shine through the windows. Suddenly, a little chubby boy came half bouncing and half running through the living room headed to our room.

"Mommy, Mommy! The sun came up! The sun came up!" He skidded to a stop when he saw me. "The sun came up! The sun came up!" Never had there been a sweeter picture of such pure delight and amazement that the sun had risen. What a great cuddle time we had that morning.

I can honestly say in all my life I have never been excited to see the sun come up. As a true night owl, I believe the work day should not officially start until at least 10:30a.m. But shame on me for not having the same appreciation for the sun coming up each day.

My sweet Lord gives me a new day, day after day. With it is a clean slate to be a better daughter to Him and a better mother to the blessings

He has entrusted to me. I want to take advantage of the time He has given me on earth with the people I love. I want to appreciate the time that goes by way too fast. Before I know it, that sweet little boy will be off to college and then his own family.

I now try each morning when I wake to say, "Good morning, Jesus." My eyes may not be open, but I think He understands my heart is screaming, "Jesus! Jesus! The sun came up! The sun came up! Thank you for another day!"

Scripture: In the morning, O Lord, you hear my voice: in the morning I lay my requests before you and wait in expectation. Psalm 5:3

Challenge: Tomorrow morning before you get out of bed say this little prayer of thanks: "Thank you, Lord, for my child(ren) and for sending me a new day to love them with Your love. Help me to acknowledge You throughout my day. Thank you that the sun came up, it's going to be a great day!" I will be saying it with you, probably with my eyes still closed.

# DAY TWO

## MUTTERING CONTENTMENT

My mother only had one child – me – so I think she is constantly flabbergasted when she is at my house at what it is like to mother four children. Sometimes it is glaringly obvious she only had one child.

Last Christmas she asked for a list of what the kids wanted for presents. I gave her some ideas for each one and then added, "Oh, can you get four red bowls?"

"Bowls?" She acted like she had never heard of such an item. I explained we have only one red bowl for cereal and all four kids want to eat out of it. Every morning it is a fight to see who wins the red bowl. Our normal chant of "you get what you get and you don't throw a fit" never works when it comes to the bowl. Mom agreed finally to send bowls, but not as Christmas presents. She would just send them immediately.

A week later four red bowls arrived in the mail. Here is the part that shouted, "I only had one child." They were all four different in shape and size. Now there was a new fight because one was much smaller and one much bigger and two were just different. Of course, food tasted the best out of the biggest bowl. So the morning battle continued and I continued the same mantra of being thankful and content with what you have.

My mantra of gratitude can be an ugly mirror if I turn it on myself some days. Am I teaching them by my example to be content and thankful because we are so truly blessed? Did they hear me muttering all last week how I would like to have a newer SUV because this one is nine years old? Yes, it runs fine; it never breaks down on us. It is in decent condition once we get the smashed granola bar out of the floor mat. But one of our friends bought a new one with such amazing bells and whistles, and the new-car smell is just intoxicating.

How would it affect them over time if they heard me whispering, "Thank you, Jesus, for a car that runs well and takes us safely where we need to go," instead of my previous muttering? I want my children to someday be able to say I am a good example. I want them to be able to say honestly they did not hear their mother complain, but that she is a thankful person.

I want more than anything for my children to someday say, "My mother is a godly woman." My blessings are too numerous to count and I really am grateful because the Lord has given me more than I deserve.

Scripture: But if we have food and clothing, we will be content with that. 1 Timothy 6:8

Challenge: I want to be a woman who is always thankful for what I do have, not murmuring for what I don't have. All mothers will agree our children learn more from what they see from us on a daily basis than from what we tell them. Tomorrow I want to play a little "count our blessings" game with my children. All of us participate by telling things we have to be thankful for – starting with being thankful for each other. Will you play with us?

# DAY THREE

## BEAUTY, INSIDE AND OUT

Four pregnancies, four c-sections, and a lack of exercise have left my midsection a little fluffier than it was before children. To make matters worse, the doctor with my first c-section did a vertical incision instead of a "bikini cut." This caused the next doctor to have to follow suit for the birth of my next three children. All four of my children have seen my up-and-down scar and know that is where they came from. Imagine the therapy they will need when they find out how babies are really born.

It has been hard for me to accept the extra pounds added over the years as well as the fact that I do not have the same figure I had as a bride. As my weight has gone up and down on the scales, so has my self-esteem.

Hollywood continues to bombard us with perfect, air-brushed bodies and thinner models. As a result, the average woman is being hit with subliminal messages that she doesn't measure up. I read a recent study stating that four out of five ten year olds are afraid of being fat. It also stated that on any given day, almost half of the women in America are on a diet and that eating disorders are at an all-time high.

After my daughter was born, I was strongly convicted how important it is for me to be her positive role model in creating a healthy self-image. If we are going to conquer the media penetrating our children's self-image, we are going to have to be strong in this battle in our home. It starts with our example.

We have to be the role model for our children in this – boy or girl. For my daughter I want her to understand her beauty comes from within her heart, the place where Jesus lives. I want her to see that a healthy self-image comes from God, not her dress size. I want my boys to someday choose a wife who knows who she is in Christ. First, they need to see it in me.

I understand it can be hard some days to see the positive in ourselves when we look in the mirror—especially when things aren't exactly in the same place they once were. We have to remember those scars, stretch-marks, or bumps are our badges of honor. They are reflective of the precious miracles God allows us to be a part of. Those little crinkles at the corners of our eyes are indicative of the joy and laughter He has given us.

God did not make any mistakes when He created you. He places high value on you as His daughter. You are the daughter of a King. The King of kings! If you remember this truth, you will walk through your day a little taller and a little more confident. You should, because you are beautiful.

Scripture: What matters is not your outer appearance – the styling of your hair, the jewelry you wear, the cut of your clothes – but your inner disposition. Cultivate inner beauty, the gentle gracious kind that God delights in. 1 Peter 3:3-4.

Challenge: Ask Jesus to show you how to foster a healthy self-image in your children – especially your daughter(s). For an entire month when you look in the mirror every morning, say out loud: "Thank you Lord for making me beautiful inside and out." I dare you. I triple-dog dare you.

# Day Four

## The Power of a Routine

I still am surprised by what my children learn from my husband and I that is not even on my mom-radar.

A perfect example of this showed up on a recent trip to the airport. It seems that every time we are flying anywhere we are running too late for comfort. We park our car, shuttle to the terminal, and as soon as we are inside, we take off in a mad dash to the ticket counter. My husband will carry our daughter on his shoulders and pull a suitcase while the boys and I are pulling our suitcases. Cooper, our youngest son, will pull his little backpack and have to run to keep up with us. We are quite a sight.

This rare occasion we got to the airport early, not having to rush to check in. However, as soon as we were inside the airport, Cooper, four years old at the time, took off at a full run. We yelled at him to come back and to walk. He was so confused. Our actions had taught him when we get to the airport – run. The poor little guy was so stressed out every time we went to the airport, and we didn't even realize we had taught him to feel this way.

It is scary to think how a routine or even how I do something with no real meaning can have such a strong impact on my children. At the same time, some routines can have such a positive effect on my children. The routine of bedtime, nighttime prayers, getting ready for school, playtime, homework, and chore time all give my children a feeling of security. A routine provides them a sense of stability.

As a child who moved multiple times between divorced parents and other family members, I longed for normalcy and routine. Each home carried a new routine or a different set of rules, thus lacking any semblance of stability in my life. I have learned this stability is invaluable to a child's well-being.

I am so thankful God has allowed me to provide routines for my children. I love how they feel stable and secure no matter what is going on in the outside world. I am trusting God this foundation grounded in constancy will give them the confidence they need to boldly spread their wings when it is time.

I am also praying for God to increase my awareness in what negative routines we are unknowingly teaching. No matter how sensitive I try to be in watching my own habits, I know I need God's help for me to really be aware. I most definitely need His help to change those habits.

If you are thinking of a routine in your home having a negative impact, you too can change it with God's help. You have been doing the best you know how. As God continues to grow us and teach us as mothers, we will continue to do a better job at this whole mommy thing. We will never be perfect parents, but aren't we blessed we have the Perfect Parent in our Father?

Scripture: To this you were called, because Christ suffered for you, leaving you an example that you should follow in his steps. 1 Peter 2:21

Challenge: I am going to be more consistent in praying for wisdom and discernment regarding things I may be unknowingly teaching my children. I encourage you to pray this too. I also challenge you, if your children are old enough to communicate at all, to ask them what routines they enjoy in your home. You might be surprised, as I was, to learn some of the things they will grudgingly admit they like.

# Day Five

## Taking Blessings for Granted

You know that feeling when you want the earth to swallow you up because you are so ashamed of what came out of your mouth and even more with what was in your heart?

We were driving to school at our usual time in the morning – late o'clock. We got stuck behind a school bus stopped in the outside lane as I was stopped in the inside lane behind two cars. It seemed to be taking forever and my eyes kept flicking from the clock to the bus to the clock. We were only about 200 yards from the school parking entrance, so close to making it on time. I could not see the lower half of the bus because of the cars in front of me but I could see a mom bent over and doing something at the back.

"Come on!" I grumbled with frustration loud enough my kids could hear. Moments later I saw the mom straighten and give a thumbs-up to the bus driver. Then the platform that was invisible to me before began to rise with a precious little boy sitting patiently in a wheel chair. His mom waved and blew kisses as he was being loaded. She stood watching and waving, throwing out a few more blown kisses, as the bus drove off before she turned to walk back home.

Traffic began to move again, but I sat paralyzed with tears in my eyes. I watched the mom walk down the sidewalk as the color of shame flooded my face and my heart broke. I wanted to run over to her and hug her and ask her forgiveness: forgiveness for taking my children for granted, forgiveness for my impatience, forgiveness for my hateful attitude because we were running late of our own accord.

But it was not really her forgiveness I wanted, it was His. I needed God's forgiveness because I had not taken the time to say thank you for our health and for our blessed family.

I hate when I let myself get so caught up in the daily rush of life that I take for granted how blessed we are. Even when it is just for a moment, it is a moment too long.

Scripture: He shall receive a blessing from the Lord and righteousness from the God of his salvation. Psalms 24:5 (NAS)

Challenge: If you are a mother blessed with children without physical or mental challenges, thank Him for feet that run, eyes that see, and ears that hear. If you are a mother the Lord entrusted to a precious child with mental or physical challenges, thank Him for trusting you with such a gift. Since He hand picked you, He must really believe in you as a mother. Thank Him for the sweet spirit inside your child which blesses your family daily. Do this each morning for an entire week while you are brushing your teeth and you won't forget to give thanks before your daily rush begins.

# Day Six

## A Little Bit of Balance

As a mother, you often find yourself going 36 different directions. So finding time to refill your own proverbial cup can seem impossible.

Balance can be a four-letter word if you are juggling a husband, children, a career and just making sure there are clean socks in everyone's drawer. Balance – well, that's a toughie! I don't think it is realistic to think we will ever find a perfect balance while we still have children at home, but it is something we have to continually strive for.

I am a firm believer God gives me all the time I need to accomplish what I need to. If I can't finish everything I need to on a regular basis, then I am doing something God did not intend for me to be taking on right now. Sometimes I have to revisit that philosophy when I find myself frequently frazzled, and I have to figure out what needs to be eliminated. It isn't that a particular activity or task is something I should never do, just maybe not during this season in my life.

As a mother, you must take care of yourself too. Too often you are, I am sure, last on your priority list. Yes, our title of Mother is very important, but the world will not stop if a load of laundry is not done *right now*. Or if you have to have sandwich night *again*.

You must learn to listen to yourself and your body and not ignore warnings you need some rejuvenation. You cannot serve your family if you are not at your best. You have to be healthy first – mentally, physically and spiritually. Those things take time, and you are worthy of that time.

It took me a long time and a lot of spiritual growth to learn this. First I had to learn the word *No* is a complete sentence. Too many times I would be asked to take on yet another project I did not have time to do. My fear of disappointing others kept me from admitting I could not accept a responsibility at the time. I have learned that when I take on more than I can handle, I am not being fair to myself or the person asking. No long explanation is needed when I cannot accept a responsibility that will take from my family or my well-being. A simple *No thank you* is a very sufficient response.

If I continued my path of overloading my plate, I would never be anything but a stress case. This would be all my children would learn and I knew I didn't want to raise a bunch of stressed-out little people. If all they saw was a stressed-out mommy, that is what they would emulate.

A saying I love and try to live by is this one I taped to my bathroom mirror: *Don't allow anything in your life that you don't want duplicated in your child's life.* It is a daily reminder to manage my responsibilities in a way that is in the best interest of my entire family.

You are the glue that holds your family together and they deserve the best *you* that you can be. You deserve to be the best *you* that you can be. When limiting your obligations, you will find you can do an even greater job on a task than when you have spread yourself too thin. And that is the real you, the woman who is extraordinary in all you do. You were made for greatness, Mom.

Scripture: There is a time for everything, and a season for every activity under heaven. Ecclesiastes 3:1

Challenge: Ponder what refreshes you mentally, physically, and spiritually, and put it into action. Is it a good movie or book? Going for a leisurely hike or walk around the neighborhood? A Bible study with girlfriends? Whatever it is, you are worth investing the time. Don't feel guilty about the time away from your family to refresh. Instead, thank Jesus for the time to renew and the ability to grow into all He intends for you to be for His glory.

# Day Seven

## Savoring the Time

Say it slowly—tick, tock, tick, tock. That is time passing BK—you know, Before Kids. Now say it as fast as you can—tick, tock, tick, tock. That is time passing WK—yes, With Kids.

When I had two babies in diapers I would often find myself wishing the time would go by faster. *I can't wait until they are potty trained. In another year we won't have to haul this diaper bag around.* It is easy to fall into a trap of wanting a season in our lives to pass a little faster. However, it would not take me too long to remember there will come a day when I would give anything to have them at home in diapers. One of my frequent prayers is for God to give me the wisdom and patience to enjoy whatever season we are in, to focus on the good and not the inconveniences.

One day it was just Anabelle and me leaving her well-check appointment at the doctor. It was a beautiful day and we had about 10 minutes to spare on our way to get her brothers from school. I had been savoring the feeling of her little three-year-old hand in mine as we walked across the parking lot. I was overwhelmed with gratitude to the Lord for letting me experience times like this with my children, and sad I don't pay closer attention to those precious little moments.

As we drove down the road I saw a park ahead with a little bridge and walking path that seemed so inviting. I whipped a u-turn and pulled up to the park. I explained to Anabelle we only had 10 minutes, but I wanted to take a walk with her. The trees and grass were so green; there was a light breeze that cooled the sunshine to the perfect temperature. I thought my heart would burst with gratitude and love at the feeling of walking along the path with my baby's hand in mine and God's beautiful creation enveloping us on all sides.

Wanting to capture the moment, I had Anabelle stop on the bridge and I took a picture of her with my phone. Now every time I look at that picture, I feel my heart expand at the memory of taking 10 minutes to smell the roses with my sweet daughter.

Being a nerd to my very core, I love to plan things. I love to look ahead and plan and make lists and prepare. It's my idea of fun. While it can be a good thing, it can also be dangerous if I forget to live in the here and now God has blessed me with.

A movie my kids love has a line in it that says, "Yesterday is history. Tomorrow is a mystery. But today is a gift, that is why it is called the present." Even though I have put the sofa pillows back on the couch seven times already today, cleaned up two spills, picked up twelve water guns, and stepped on four little metal cars, today truly is a gift.

I know some days can be daunting and draining. Some nights we fall into bed so glad the day is over. Despite the aggravations we encounter, it is important to savor the season when we still have them under our roof. A friend once told me you only have 18 summers with your children. I am down to only seven with my oldest son. And the clock is ticking.

I am committed to being more diligent in savoring the little moments that make life more precious. I have a feeling it is those little moments my children will remember most too.

Scripture: But I trust in you, O Lord; I say, "You are my God." My times are in your hands. Psalms 31:14-15a

Challenge: I am going to find at least one thing to do with my children that is out of the ordinary. Maybe it will be an activity we have not done together in a long time. Some of my children's favorite things are having dinner by candlelight, going on a picnic in the mountains, and roasting marshmallows outside over the fire pit. I hope you will commit to one new activity you can do with your child this week. Be sure to snap a photo of it. Your heart will grow warm each time you reflect on your new memory.

# Day Eight

## Blessed, Not Too Busy

No matter whom you talk to or what their occupation, you will often hear the same story, "We are just so busy." Time after time I hear women complain they do not have time to do what they need to. Sometimes there is a silent competition of *I am busier than you are.* I believe this *busy syndrome* is really not in our daily lives, but in our minds.

Women of previous generations were no less busy than we are today. They often had larger families to tend to and cooked three square meals a day, never grabbing fast food. They washed their clothes by hand and hung them on a line to dry, not tossed them in a dryer. They mended socks and made clothes for their families, unlike our buy and toss practices today.

Many worked outside the home as teachers, nurses and other professions. They had church socials, quilting groups, and took meals to sick friends. Yet they also took time to sit on the porch with their families or neighbors. They took tea and muffins to a friend and had face-to-face relational time.

It is unfortunate we have allowed martyrdom to creep into our attitudes about all we have to do. We look at the responsibilities of our families as a yoke instead of a blessing.

I come from a long, proud line of martyrs, and for many years I carried on this female trait in my home. My attitude was a feeling of constantly being overwhelmed and a victim of too many responsibilities. This attitude led to negativity, frustration, and overwhelming stress.

Thankfully, I began to see this state of mind and responsibility overload was self-inflicted. God had trusted me to care for our beautiful family and make our home a safe haven. I viewed it as a burden, not the gift it is.

How can I ask God to bless my family and me personally when I don't have a thankful heart for what He has given to me? My commitment to myself, my family, and more importantly, to God is to release myself from this busy state of mind. I will be grateful for every second I have with my family and friends, and I will enjoy the material things He has given us. I certainly do not want to behave as if I am too busy to bless others. And I do not want to behave like I am too busy to appreciate all my blessings.

Webster's dictionary defines appreciate as "recognizing the value or quality of; to value highly." I want to *appreciate* the Lord for all I have. We often appreciate another when they show us an act of kindness or bless us, but do we appreciate God for His blessings and acts of kindness towards us? Let's truly appreciate Him.

Scripture: Many women do noble things, but you surpass them all. Proverbs 31:29

Challenge: When you feel a seed of frustration or become overwhelmed tomorrow, stop and make a mental list of what you can appreciate God for in your life. Whisper a prayer of appreciation for all He has given you – most importantly, your family. Make a commitment to not be too busy in your mind so you can hear Him speak to you more clearly.

# DAY NINE

## SPEAKING BLESSINGS

The Bible says there is life and death in the power of the tongue. Proverbs 18:21 in *The Message* says, "Words kill, words give life; they're either poison or fruit – you choose."

This verse is a powerful reminder of the weight my words can have on myself and my family. The scary part is I can choose whether they are poisonous or fruitful. Do they give hope or discouragement? It can be easy to control my tongue when I am in a happy mood or everything is running smoothly. What about when I lose my patience or become angry?

Throughout the Bible there are illustrations of the impact of our words. One great example is Genesis 27:21-40. The father, Isaac, was tricked into giving his blessing to Jacob, his younger son, instead of Esau, his first born. On his deathbed, Isaac spoke his blessings to Jacob in the presence of the Lord, and once they were spoken, Isaac could not take back the words. When Esau found out his father had mistakenly given the blessing to Jacob, he burst out with a "loud and bitter cry[1]." Even Isaac trembled and shook violently, because he understood he could not take back the impact of his words.

As mothers, we have not only a great influence over our children, but the enormous responsibility to use our words to give life, to give hope.

We have a family friend who spent several years telling not just his daughter, but friends and family, that his daughter was on a path of destruction. He began speaking these words long before there were signs of rebellion.

Today his daughter has been in and out of prison and is a drug addict, and he is certain that he was right all along. I don't know how this young girl would have turned out if her dad had spoken words of hope and encouragement instead, but I have to wonder what impact they had on her choices.

I know sometimes there is no evident explanation when a child rebels and walks away from God. However, it is our God-given responsibility to use our words for encouragement and love.

On my journey of learning God's Word and growing spiritually, I have learned one of the ways my faith is built is by what I hear. This started me reciting aloud scriptures which give me encouragement and hope in Christ. It had a strong impact in teaching me who God is and who He made me to be. I know if I had truly known who I was in Christ when I was younger, I would have made many different choices. While I am thankful for the messy path that led me to where I am today, it is my desire for my children to make fewer mistakes than I did.

The realization that my spiritual growth came more effectively through hearing the Word led me to speaking blessings and scriptures to my children. Helping them find their confidence from the Lord and not from man starts with my words to them.

When each one was a small baby, I began whispering scripture to their tiny ears, blessing them with my words. Today I still whisper to them at bedtime, sometimes even after they are sleeping.

I tell them they are fearfully and wonderfully made[2] and God loves them so much that He knows the very number of hairs on their little heads[3]. I remind them they can do all things through Christ who gives them strength[4]. I tell them the Lord will bless them and everything they put their hands to[5], and how much Jesus loves them[6]. I assure them He has great plans for them, to give them a future and a hope[7]. I know they may still be too young to understand what I am saying, but I know I am planting a seed that will grow with them.

Scripture: May the words of my mouth and the meditation of my heart be pleasing in your sight, O Lord, my Rock and my Redeemer. Psalms 19:14

Challenge: No matter how old your children are, I pray you will continue to speak positive, life-giving words to them every day. Let us both find something new we can compliment our children on. Let us be challenged together to speak faith and optimism and joy into our children's hearts. They may roll their eyes at us as they get older, but our words will have a deep impact on their future choices. Let's partner together to raise up a new generation who knows who they are in Christ and are equipped to make a great impact on our world.

[1]Genesis 27:34; [2] Psalm 139:14; [3] Matthew 10:30; [4] Philippians 4:13; [5] Deuteronomy 28:8; [6] John 3:16; [7] Jeremiah 29:11

# DAY 10

## DOING THEIR PART

My children hear the word *chores* and a barrage of eye-rolling and groaning unleashes from their bodies until they are rolling around on the floor like they are physically wounded. Not that I am saying they are a little dramatic or anything. However, I do think they would check the *yes* box if they were polled on the breaking of child labor laws in our home.

What they do not realize now, though, is they are growing into responsible and independent little people. As soon as they could walk, I started teaching them how to pick up toys and put them in a basket. By three years of age, they all made their own beds. It wasn't always pretty, but it produced many proud moments. As I showered them with praise, their little smiles grew from ear to ear.

Also when they were three years old, they helped me unload the dishwasher. I would remove all glass and any sharp items, and then I would let them pick up the dish from the racks and hand it to me. It took a little longer, but they were proud they were able to help Mommy. Many a preschool or church teacher has complimented my children on always picking up the toys when class is over.

Now that they are growing older, they like to pretend they hate doing chores. But the two oldest let it slip one time that they wanted to learn to do more chores around the house, such as laundry and cooking. I watch their little faces when they tackle something new and see the pride and the growth of their independence surfacing in their determined eyes.

We recently went on a family camping trip with another family and their two preteen children. As it was time to pack up our sites, these two children were sitting and watching the work being done. My husband and I were assigning age-appropriate duties to all of our children, from the 4 year old to the 10 year old.

On the trip home, my oldest shared his observation of the two children not helping and this developed into a great discussion. I explained to him how his contributions were benefiting him.

First of all, he is part of our team—our family—and it is his duty to contribute to the team. And, as a team player, he is able to see the hard work his dad and I put into these types of activities.

Lastly, I told him that he is learning important skills he can someday use when camping with his college friends or teaching his own children. It was a great teaching moment and I was proud of him that he understood and saw the benefits of his contributions.

Because our children do chores, they are learning how to do tasks they will need to know their entire lives. They also play important roles in the running of our household. In addition, they are learning character qualities, such as seeing a job through to the end. They will be able to experience the satisfaction of doing a job well. Equally important, they are learning to appreciate others when something is done for them, because they have experienced it and can see the work it takes.

I am most proud they are learning independence. This independence blesses us as parents because they are making a great contribution to our home. And they are blessed with a high self-esteem and sense of value because they are able to do things themselves without help from an adult.

Some mothers worry about teaching their child too young, while others feel they have missed the opportunity with their teenager. While it is challenging at first to cultivate that independence, it makes a great difference in their futures. When the time comes to leave the nest, it will be an easier step for them because they are responsible and independent young adults. Any stage on their path to adulthood is an opportunity to learn those qualities.

Many have asked me if I believe children should be given an allowance for doing chores. While I can't tell you what is right for your family, I can tell you we do not give allowances for chores in our home. I believe in an allowance, but I also believe doing chores is what one does because he gets to live in my house. My children groan and roll their eyes when I deny payment for taking out the trash, but I can also see they feel like a very valuable part of our team.

My husband and I never let an occasion pass to tell them how important they are in our family and how proud we are of them. A lavishing of love and praise helps the eye rolling and groans pass quickly into laughter and team work. I know someday they will thank us. Just not for a long time.

Scripture: Even a child is known by his actions, by whether his conduct is pure and right. Proverbs 20:11

Challenge: If you do not already have a system in place in your home, I challenge you to create a list of age-appropriate duties to place on the refrigerator; then implement your plan. If your children are toddlers, a calendar to put stickers on is a fun reward for them when they help you. For your older children, explain to them the benefits of their contributions. No matter the age or job, lavish them with praise and appreciation. They are a valuable part of your team.

# Day 11

## The Comparison Game

I have a friend who is just gorgeous. Not only that, she is physically fit, business savvy, and intelligent. She has a beautiful home, a sweet husband and she, herself, has a heart of gold. She always seems so put together and sharp. She is not the person you want to hang out with when you have PMS or a bad hair day.

We knew each other for a couple of years before we became more than friendly acquaintances. Honestly, I was intimidated by her and I was not completely comfortable around her for a long time. I was intimidated because I subconsciously compared myself to her.

One day I heard her tell another person that when she first met me she was intimidated by me. She said she felt like I *had it all together* and it made her feel like a mess. I could not believe my ears.

Comparing ourselves to others seems to be a sport women excel in. Even if we don't readily admit it, it happens much too often. There is always a mom who looks like she stepped out of a magazine when dropping her children off at school in the morning. It's too early to look that good, how does she do it? She drives the clean, shiny SUV in front of you and you can smell her new-car-new-leather fragrance back in your dusty, old ride.

But, the worst comparison game is when you start comparing your children to another mother's children.

With three wiggly boys, including one who often acts on his first impulse, this is a dangerous area for me. I remember sitting at a banquet where I was being recognized as the Young Mother of Nevada. It was a beautiful brunch in an elegant setting with several people giving nice speeches. My boys, ages three to nine at the time, were trying to contain the ants in their pants but with little success. I looked around at the other children sitting quietly and seeming to pay attention to the speakers. Although my boys were not being loud or disruptive, I wanted them to sit perfectly behaved like the other children. What should have been a wonderful moment for me was almost ruined by me comparing my children to others.

There have been times I have felt inadequate because I would see another mother demonstrate endless patience with her child while I was about to explode with my own. Comparing ourselves to other women is a useless and treacherous act that will put us on a path to unhappiness.

When we compare ourselves to others, we are allowing roots of jealousy, discouragement, discontentment, and insecurity to begin to grow within us. These are emotions that will never allow us a moment of peace. In addition, when we are constantly envious of others, we can never be truly happy for someone else's good fortune or success.

As a Christian mother, you must know who you are in Christ's eyes. He created you just the way you are to use you as He planned. He did not make any mistakes with you. You also have to know He hand-picked your children for you to mother. Did you ever stop to think about why He gave you the children you have and why He gave me the children I have and so on?

He knew He had already equipped you to successfully raise the children He trusted you with. In Genesis 15:4-5, God took Abraham outside his tent and told him to look up at the stars. God told Abraham that the number of stars would be the number of his descendants. From then on, every time Abraham looked at those stars, they served as a reminder of God's promise.

In the same way God gave Abraham a visual reminder, He also gave you a visual reminder. Each time you look at your children, they should serve as a reminder that God believes in your abilities to be just the right parent for your child. There is always going to be someone who has a nicer home, smarter children, or a newer car than you. But you have to know there is always going to be someone looking at you, thinking you have thinner thighs and a cuter hairstyle than they do.

God wants us all to know our confidence comes from Him, not from things of this world. He wants you to walk in His light and experience contentment and joy with the blessings He has given you. You are much too valuable to Him to be going through life feeling insecure, jealous, or discouraged.

As role models in our homes, it is important for us to be an example of contentment, not comparison, for our children. I know none of us want our children feeling inadequate and fearing they *don't measure up* to their peers. But I do believe if they constantly see that being demonstrated in us, that is what they will do as well.

Mom, the only person you need to be comparing yourself to is the beautiful woman in the mirror. Are you being the best *you* God made you to be? When you are being the best *you* that God intended, then you are free to love and appreciate others for whom God made them to be. Not only will you be free from the bait of jealousy and discontentment, you will likely develop some lasting friendships. And heaven knows we need those.

Scripture: Each one should test his own actions. Then he can take pride in himself, without comparing himself to somebody else. Galatians 6:4

Challenge: Now don't tell me no—it is important you do this. Make a list of five things you like about yourself physically, then five things you like about yourself in general. Add five things you are good at, followed by five things you have accomplished this far in your life. Just slip this in your sock drawer if you don't want anyone to see it, but where it is handy for you to glance at in the mornings or when you find yourself in the comparison game. For those bold mothers, tape it to your bathroom mirror and look at it every morning. You will have 20 positive things about yourself to serve as a reminder of the magnificent wonders of God's creation. He did good, Sister!

# DAY 12

## JOY OF THE LORD

I remember all the songs about the joy of the Lord that I used to sing growing up in children's church. The words proclaimed the joy of the Lord is our strength and told of the joy of the Lord down in our hearts. Today you will find hundreds of books, both Christian and secular, about finding happiness—this evasive mystery very few have. The saddest part is that a lack of joy is prevalent in our churches as well, the very place that should be the role model for joy and contentment.

I am blessed with some very godly family members who have spent years building their faith. They serve faithfully in their churches and have a great knowledge and understanding of God's holy word. But, one person comes to my mind frequently because there is a lack of joy in this person's worship. I know there is a love and reverence for the Lord, but there seems to be more obligation than pleasure in the service.

It breaks my heart because I know there is great excitement in a relationship with Jesus Christ. I serve a very fun God! Yes, God is omnipotent and worthy of all praise and glory. We are nothing without Him and He is to be revered and feared. But while He is my Savior, He too is my Father. He is a Daddy to me, the only Daddy I have had many times in my life.

In the same way my husband does things for our children, Jesus does things for me just to make me smile. He cares about everything I care about. What is important to me, no matter how insignificant to another, is important to Him. Because I am important to Him.

God has been so full of surprises in my life that I have learned being in a relationship with Him is never boring. Sometimes He brings me to tears of humility, and other times He brings me to screams of "Woot! Woot!"

Sometimes I clap my hands and give Him a standing ovation. And not just a golf clap, but a downright *You-are-so-amazing-I-am-so-humbled* resounding clap. God has surprised my husband and me with job promotions, bonuses, and raises we did not know were coming. He has blessed us with unexpected checks when we were between jobs. He has blessed me with recognition and honor that was completely out of the blue, and promoted me in front of those trying to cause strife in my life.

I share funny, silly little moments with Jesus, just like I would with an earthly father. When I go shopping, I frequently nab a front row parking spot, no matter how crowded the parking lot. It is like a little game between Jesus and me, and I will say I am highly favored, then I clap for Jesus just for fun. My friends and family think it is funny and are amazed too. And we laugh and clap for Jesus together.

Jesus is always with us, but too often we may only recognize it in the hard times. He is faithful to comfort us and give us strength in the good times too. He hurts when we hurt, but He also shares in our joys. And more importantly, He is our source of joy.

Psalms 97:11 tells us, "He sheds us with joy." The Message states it like this: "Light-seeds are planted in the souls of God's people, Joy-seeds are planted in good heart-soil." There will be times of trouble and sadness while we are here on earth. Happiness is a feeling we may not have during difficult circumstances, but we can have His joy and contentment in our hearts all of the time.

You may be wondering what this has to do with being a mother? I believe the joy of the mother sets the tone for the home. The old saying, "when momma ain't happy, ain't nobody happy," carries much truth. My children will have a hard time learning God's joy if they do not see it modeled daily.

One of the most important things I want to teach my children is to experience a true relationship with Jesus—not just to know the Bible and follow the commandments, but a real relationship. I want my children to know the joy of Jesus, and to enjoy His presence so much they can hardly contain it. I want them to have those moments with Him that make them want to scream "Woot! Woot!"

It took me many years into adulthood to come to where I am and I know He is not finished with me yet. Fortunately, He is still working on us all. It is my heart's desire that you also experience His joy constantly. It makes the fun times more fun and the mundane times less tedious. It even makes unloading the dishwasher more bearable.

Scripture: You have loved righteousness and hated wickedness; therefore God, your God, has set you above your companions by anointing you with the oil of joy. Hebrews 1:9

Challenge: Take a few moments to recall a fun surprise or an unexpected blessing. Acknowledge that all good things come from Jesus. Commit to recognizing immediately the fun little blessings Jesus gives you each day. And next time you grab a front row parking spot, clap your hands and declare you are a highly favored child of God. I promise you will giggle and feel His joy.

# Day 13

## Always Better with a Buddy

My cousin and I have a rule we have lived by since the day we were old enough to count calories. When we eat dessert together, it doesn't count. I think it is one of the smarter rules we have ever created. But isn't it true that everything is better with a buddy?

Being a mom can be easier with a buddy too. I know you are deep in the trenches of mommyville every day. Sometimes it can be a deep pit when you are buried by a pile of dirty clothes and unfolded clean ones. But doesn't it seem a lighter load when you have a friend to share your day with? One who is buried in her own home and really gets what you are going through.

I remember the days when my husband would come home from work to a house covered with toys and burp cloths, clean clothes piled on the bed, dinner barely started, and my makeup-less face framed by a disheveled ponytail. He would walk the obstacle course of stuff to greet me with a kiss, and he would not say a word about the condition of the house.

Still the words could come gushing out of me (with a hint of mint as I had only brushed my teeth two hours before for the first time that day), "I barely sat down all day!" The tornado zone surrounding me really did look like I had done nothing all day, but I had not stopped working since crawling out of bed that morning.

It was such a relief to talk to my girlfriends with small children and know they had had the very same day. And necessity being the mother of all invention, I began to develop partnerships and little systems that helped me run my household a little better.

My dessert-sharing cousin is the best person I've ever known at keeping absolutely zero clutter. Her house always looks as if it is staged for potential buyers. She has coached me about ridding my house of things that don't make me happy. While I was always good at packing up clothes to give away, I was very poor at getting rid of the knick-knacks and items around my house I no longer wanted or needed. Especially if it was given to me as a gift.

One day her words impacted me greatly when I was complaining of feeling overwhelmed. She said "If it drives you crazy, get rid of it. It doesn't matter how much you spent on it, if it doesn't bring you joy get it out of your house." Boy, did I take that to heart. I went around and boxed up so much stuff to donate that I filled three large boxes and several big trash bags. The kids began hiding from me because I was on such a mission of giving things away. When the non-profit came to pick up my donation, I felt so much lighter. A cluttered house can make a cluttered mind. Now I had some sanity back.

Then a friend and I began to share work days every week or two. She would come to my house and help me with a project, clean, or whatever I needed. Then I would go to her house and work in her yard or complete her to-do lists. We worked hard while our children played together and it was such a fulfilling day as we accomplished our task at hand.

As my children are growing, our lives become more hectic as I chauffeur them after school to acting class or sports or church functions. And the 5 o'clock panic was always a stress for me. We eat out infrequently, so coming up with new ideas for dinner was always the most frustrating process. After talking with a couple of moms, I found I was not alone in this. So we partnered up for menu ideas.

We each had to make a list of a week's worth of meal ideas with any recipes that may be needed and e-mail them to each other. By doing this we would have three week's worth of meal ideas. While some things I may have on my menu, their children would not eat–such as sauerkraut– we still had ideas we could build upon. Even if we had sandwich night scheduled on the menu, we would include it in our list. It was not only helpful; it was fun to see what others had on their family menu.

I am sure you have a buddy or two you share great ideas and helpful tips with. Thank God for our friends whom we can share our lives with and those we can encourage as well as be encouraged by. We are all in this together and we need each other, especially to make the mundane a lot more fun. Let's link arms and conquer that laundry room together.

Scripture: My command is this: Love each other as I have loved you. John 15:12

Challenge: If you are a new mom, I challenge you to find a mother with older children and borrow some of her secrets to sanity. She has walked your path and probably has many pearls of wisdom to share with you. If you are a more seasoned mom, there is someone who needs you. Whether it is your words of encouragement or how you juggled all the tasks over the years, you have much to offer. I promise when you reach out to another mother, you both will be blessed.

# Day 14

## You are a Princess

After three perfect, rowdy baby boys, we received the surprise of our lives with a bundle of pink. For several days after Anabelle was born, my husband and I were so in shock that when someone said *sister* or *daughter,* we just stared at each other.

What drove me crazy though was that everyone just assumed I wanted a girl. And the truth of it was—I didn't. I wanted four boys. Strangers in the grocery would stop me to say, "You finally got your girl," as if I had tried and failed three times to have a girl. It didn't resonate well with me, especially in the midst of post-partum hormones.

The reality was that I was very afraid of having a girl, for many reasons. The biggest reason, however, was I felt completely ill-equipped to raise a daughter. I was afraid of all the possible mistakes I could make in guiding her because I had made such poor choices through my teens and early 20's.

Although I attended church my entire life, as a teenager and young adult I still had not learned the value God placed on me as His daughter. My self-confidence and choices were based on man's opinion of me, not what God had already determined. This lack of knowledge and understanding that I was a child of God led to many heartbreaks and much regret. How could I ever protect an innocent baby girl from the same path I had traveled?

It took me some time to see He trusted me with this precious little girl. He also knew the healing she would bring to me, just by her very being. It was an example of God doing one deed to serve many.

Yes, it is my responsibility to love, guide, teach, and serve her first and foremost. But God gave me more than just the gift of a daughter; He used her to give me healing and hope. He humbled me by choosing me to raise this child. Now I am relying heavily on Him to show me each day how to be an example for her to follow.

I am passionate about her learning who God says she is. When I am whispering words of blessing and scripture as I tuck her in at night, I am careful to tell her that her value comes only from God and she is the child of a King. I tell her it doesn't matter what any boy or girl may say someday, her worth has already been set by Christ and He loves her and values her like no other.

I know in my heart that if she really knows this truth deep within, she will not make the same choices I did. While she may make mistakes along the way, she is going to seek God's approval, not man's approval. Although she is only four years old, I see she is already learning these words I say to her.

It is a sweet, intimate time we share together as we cuddle on her bed and she strokes my cheek while I talk softly to her. I am so grateful God has placed her and me on this journey together to learn and grow in Christ despite the years between our ages.

It is never too early nor too late to learn how important you are to Him. He made you in His image. He created you the way He wanted you to be because He had a specific purpose only you could fulfill. What you may see as a weakness in yourself, God can use for His glory.

You were hand-picked by Him to be the mother to your children. He sees everyday how much you love them and how hard you work for their best interest. None of your sacrifices go unnoticed by Him.

And He wants you to remember you, too, are a child of a King. You are a princess. You are important to Him and He loves you so very much. He wants to be your strength on the tough days and to share your joys in your happy times. As valuable as your children are to you, you too, are that valuable to Him. Dare I say, even more so.

Scripture: If you belong to Christ, then you are Abraham's seed, and heirs according to the promise. Galatians 3:29

Challenge: Tomorrow is a new day. If you have battled with regret, fear, or lack of confidence, now is the time to set it at the foot of the cross. You will start tomorrow with the knowledge that you are a most prized treasure to your Father, the King. I encourage you to start searching the Bible for scriptures to enforce this. Read them out loud and commit them to memory so you can recite them daily.

# Day 15

## Ideas for You, Mom

I love sharing ideas with other mothers. I have grown to believe mothers are the most ingenious humans walking the planet. So I want to share a few ideas my friends and I have shared with each other. Some may not be age-appropriate for your children and you may have to tweak some, but you are a genius after all, so it will be no problem for you.

Create a mini-bag for toys to be played with only when you are at a restaurant. Include crayons and mini-books, miniature sized legos, or small puzzles. Older children enjoy word puzzle books. Leave the bag in the back of your car and it will be handy when you go out to eat.

Use the bottom drawer of your refrigerator for a snack drawer for your children. Prepare pre-filled snack bags of carrots or sliced apples or string cheese, cups of yogurt and applesauce, and miniature water bottles. Children of all ages can grab their own healthy snack.

Flour tortillas make every food more fun. Use them instead of bread for a fancy grilled cheese, or smear peanut butter and jelly on them and roll them up. For a fun dessert, spread peanut butter on one, sprinkle the middle with mini-chocolate chips and marshmallows, and roll up like a burrito. Put in foil and heat in oven until melted. These are also a great item for camping.

A favorite dip for fruit is vanilla yogurt mixed with peanut butter. You can mix to your preferred consistency and it is great for dipping apples and bananas.

Thin pretzel sticks are a fun food for children. Slice up apples or cheese chunks and they can stab the food with the pretzel. They can also scoop up peanut butter or mustard with them.

Put a calendar on your refrigerator for everyone to write on. Teach your children to write in game times, class parties, and social events. If you have more than one child, you may assign a different ink color to each one. Not only will this help your whole family know what each one is doing, it will teach them organization skills for their entire lives.

If you are teaching your toddler his colors, use M&M's. Every time he gets one right, he gets to eat it. It is a fun and yummy way to learn.

When camping or staying in a hotel, take along a couple of glow sticks that are activated by bending and shaking. You can then tie them from the ceiling of the tent, or the top of a piece of furniture in the hotel. They are an inexpensive and fun way to provide a night light for younger children.

Scripture: Sons are a heritage from the Lord, children a reward from him. Psalms 127:3

Challenge: One of the best gifts you can give a new mother or mother-to-be is savvy ideas to help her in her new role. Maybe you can create a little notebook of your own with these tips along with your ideas to give her. Include some quick and easy recipes to complete the perfect gift. Use your social media page to seek out your friends' helpful hints too.

# Day 16

## Something Just for You

I know this may be a rare thing for you to hear. Perhaps you have never heard another human utter these words since labor was over. Here it is: *Right now, this is all about you.*

I don't want to talk about your miniature people or your title of mother. I want to talk solely about you. There was a hit song years ago that said, "What have you done for me lately?" I ask you, "What have you done for you lately?" And I am not talking about just sneaking away to potty by yourself. Or stealing a bubble bath.

When is the last time you challenged yourself? The last time you stepped out of your comfort zone? As age 40 approached, I began to have my own mini mid-life crisis, so to speak. I kept thinking how I only had a year to accomplish goals I had set decades before. Any goals that I had achieved were blurry in the background of my mind. I wanted to do something I had dreamed about.

After thinking about it for about 26 seconds, I remembered I had wanted to run a marathon. So after 10 years of running only to hide from my children, I again took up running as a sport. Not wanting to get too ambitious, I signed up for the half-marathon just five months away.

Fortunately, I had some friends who were experienced in running races, and they shared their tips and experiences with me. Unfortunately, as the race drew closer I became sick and was not able to run more than six miles at one time. But how hard could it be, right? It's just running that same 6 miles twice with a little tacked on to the end to sum up to 13.1 miles.

So at 39 ½ years old in 40 degree weather, I lined up at 6am with about 20,000 other fools. I hit mile one and my self-talk was great. I hit mile six and was still glad to be out there. Mile eight flashed by and I started to think that if I stopped running I would not be able to start again. And this is when, I am sure, many of the full-marathon runners were crossing the finish line after their 26.2 mile stint.

Mile 10 came and I began swearing at myself for not still being home in my warm bed, and I decided to walk. The pain was now killing me, and I walked and jogged and limped for two more miles. With one mile to go, I seriously considered hailing a cab. But I was so close to accomplishing something I set out to do. This was about me!

With about a half mile left in the race, I pushed through the excruciating pain and began to jog again. Yes, my pride would not let me walk across the finish line while so many people watched. Sometimes pride can be a positive force. I had done it. Of course, hours later I was lying in ice packs crying. But I had done it.

I know there are dreams you once had, now collecting dust on a shelf somewhere. If you got do-overs, what would you do? A different career? Learn to dance? Take a cake-decorating class? Take up rock climbing? Write a book? Travel?

It is so important for you to embrace those dreams and goals inside you. God didn't give you those dreams by accident. Sometimes you need to do the very thing that scares you. God will enable you to achieve that which he expects you to attempt. Don't wait until you are an empty-nest mom to nurture your dreams and goals; do them now while your children are watching. You will set a powerful example for your children as they see their mom doing something outside the box.

It's not too late. Sign up for an on-line course. Start saving your pennies for the trip of your dreams. Volunteer to lead the next Bible study. Make up your mind you are going to do something just for you and your personal growth. I know spare time is a luxury, but the time you will spend on yourself is an investment. It's not a waste of time. You deserve it. This one act can be all about you. I am not giving up on my marathon goal. What is the race you want to run in?

Scripture: Be very careful, then, how you live – not as unwise but as wise, making the most of every opportunity. Ephesians 5:15-16a

Challenge: I know there is something in the back of your mind that comes up often but you ignore. Start tomorrow the action steps to pursue that goal. Do any research you need to, inquire with the right people and find out what your first steps are. Do not procrastinate another day in stretching yourself outside your comfort zone. Your dreams are too valuable not to pursue. You are too valuable.

# Day 17

## Let Go or Bubble Wrap

The two little words *letting go* are something we all have heard, most have said, and many refuse to do. Letting go can take on so many different meanings. We usually apply the words to the time our children leave the nest, but *letting go* actually starts at day one.

My first letting go experience was the simple act of letting someone else hold my new, perfect baby boy. I would stare–glare–at the person holding him until the moment I could take him back again. Allowing that same little boy to spend the night with a friend many years later was more exercise of my letting-go muscles. I still workout those muscles daily with all four children all at different phases of their lives.

On our family camping trip this weekend, Anabelle and I were holding hands on our hike. Hiking down a steep hill toward our camp site, she adamantly pulled her little four-year-old hand out of mine and began to slowly step down the hill. I insisted she hold my hand and I tried to grab her hand back because I was afraid of her falling.

"I can do it, Mommy," she said. Then pronouncing each word with emphasis she said again, "I can do it." Ouch.

I want to wrap all four of them in bubble wrap and keep them sheltered from the world in the safety of my own home. But I also want them to walk boldly but cautiously throughout their lives, relying on God, stretching and growing under His watch. Mostly I want to wrap them in bubble wrap.

It is getting harder for me as my oldest is becoming a teenager. One of my closest friends, Susie, sent me an email I know many mothers can relate to. She wrote:

> "One of the most bittersweet moments is watching your child become a teenager. It is so difficult to let them go. It is difficult because you have to place them back in God's arms and hope that you have prepared them to enter adulthood. You can no longer have the control you once had when they were little, knowing where they are and what they are doing. As they become teenagers it is so easy for them to fall under attack of the devil and this is frightening. This never really occurred to me when he was younger."

I have learned with each season of our children's lives, there are new ways we have to learn to let go a little. Whether it be a toddler stretching his independence and learning to do something new at home or a teenager with a new driver's license and a craving for freedom, we are learning to balance letting go while keeping boundaries in check.

A wonderful mother and mentor from my church once told me you do not have to "lose your teenagers" like many profess. She has raised three wonderful children into adulthood, and she said she loved the teenage years with her children. This was music to my ears and I hope to yours as well.

When our children can try new things under our watch, we have the ability to influence and direct their steps as we are building their confidence. They need to know at every age, we believe in them. We are giving them the opportunity to build our trust as we are teaching them the meaning of being a trustworthy person. When we allow them the opportunity to make a wise decision on their own, we have the occasion to give praise and appreciation for whom they are becoming.

You are doing such a wonderful job raising up your godly little man or woman and I know this is not an easy part of parenting. I do believe we all can learn to let go a little more when we need to with encouragement from each other and much prayer. Every day I am learning to rely more on Him, the perfect Parent. But I am still learning, and I still have the bubble wrap handy.

Scripture: I will instruct you and teach you in the way you should go; I will counsel you and watch over you. Psalms 32:8

Challenge: As you pray over your children, ask God to show you in which areas you need greater boundaries and in which areas you need to let go a little more. Continue seeking God for the answers and be patient with yourself as you grow and learn as a mother. God knows you are receiving on-the-job training and He believes in your abilities. As our teenagers grow into adults, they are faced with greater challenges that can affect them for the rest of their lives. Commit to praying diligently over their choices and ask God to help you build stronger communication between you and your teen.

# Day 18

## Billy's Scars

"You can kiss me on the cheek without the scars."

Isn't it funny how a seemingly insignificant conversation from your childhood can impact you so greatly as an adult? I had forgotten about this incident for over two decades until one day it came back to my mind and has stayed with me ever since.

When I was ten years old, I had a playmate named Billy, who had been burned and had scars up and down one side of his face. I can still picture so clearly the brown grass and falling leaves around us. We were crouched down outside the barn wall trying to hide from the chilly breeze. As the sun was dropping, so was the temperature.

Billy asked, "Will you kiss me? I don't think I will ever get married because of my scars and I will never get kissed by a girl."

When I hesitated for what seemed like a long time, he quietly said, "Please? You can kiss me on the cheek without the scars."

So after a longer moment of hesitation, I said, "Okay," and then quickly pecked his cheek without the scars.

Thirty years later, I want so much to grab that ten-year-old boy's face and kiss all his scars. My own ten-year-old immaturity did not yet have the wisdom to understand what a poignant moment this would be in my life. Billy grew up to be a handsome man with a beautiful family of his own and I doubt he even remembers that fall evening by the barn.

The question which continues to plague me is, how many of us are walking around with scars that are affecting our lives? But unlike Billy, very few of us wear our scars on the outside where others can see them. While we smile bravely facing our friends and family, we are being weighed down by the scars on our hearts.

From the time my parents divorced when I was 5 until I left for college, I moved many times throughout the years. Not only did I move to different houses, I moved between my parents and other family members. I longed for the closeness of a traditional family and the security of being with two parents in one home. Because it was so painful to be constantly uprooted, I vowed that my own children would never feel the lack of stability and security that I grew up with.

These wounds greatly impacted not only my marriage in the early years, but also my parenting. I set unrealistic expectations for myself and my husband. It took an enormous commitment from both of us to get through my fears and into a healthy, happy marriage. For my husband, an argument between us was just that—an argument. For me, an argument was a divorce and a move.

When I had children, I almost worked myself to death to ensure everything was *perfect*. I wanted every holiday to be a Norman Rockwell painting. I pressured myself to make sure every meal was homemade, every birthday cake personally baked and decorated, and every party more elaborate than the last. The motives behind what I did for my family were not driven by simple desire or joy, but from lack of healing and understanding.

Overcoming my past and receiving God's healing did not happen overnight, but took years of God's grace and mercy. I am a strong advocate for breaking the cycle of abuse, neglect or dysfunctional parenting, and I have learned how unhealed wounds can push us to extreme actions and expectations that can never be fulfilled.

If you are harboring pain from your past, whether it was self-inflicted or you were wounded by another, it is time to be healed completely from it. Jesus never intended for us to carry those burdens alone. His mercies are fresh and new everyday and His word promises us that He will bind up our wounds and heal our broken hearts. Your children are not expecting perfection from you; by God's grace your children love you just as you are. You deserve God's best, and a hurting heart is not His best. He wants to heal your heart. Whether it be a small ache or a gaping hole of anguish, He wants to heal it for you.

Scripture: Praise be to the God and Father of our Lord Jesus Christ, the Father of compassion and the God of all comfort, who comforts us in all our troubles so that we can comfort those in any trouble with the comfort we ourselves have received from God. 2 Corinthians 1:3-4

Challenge: If you have carried a burden alone any length of time, that is too long. I encourage you to prayerfully seek someone you can share your pain with. It may be your husband, a pastor, or a mentor in your church. If you have many issues you are trying to overcome, I highly recommend a Christian counselor you can be honest with. He or she can give you a compassionate ear and help you work through your troubles. It takes courage to seek someone out to talk to and pray with, but you are a courageous woman. If you are one that has victory over your own hurts, you could be the answer to someone's prayer by giving a compassionate ear and partnering in prayer with them.

# DAY 19

## LAUGH IT UP

Don't you savor those moments when your child says or does something so sweet and extraordinary that your pride could explode your body? You have that fleeting but celebrated feeling of "maybe I'm not doing such a bad job here." I love those moments. Then as soon as I dislocate my shoulder from patting myself on the back, he or she completely humbles me.

I guess it is just part of the cycle of motherhood. But despite the trials and messiness that motherhood can sometimes be, most of the time I find it to be the most fun job in the world.

I remember when I was in college–years before having a family of my own–sitting at a stop light next to a mini-van with a family inside. I saw the mom and the dad in the front seat and a boy and a girl around ages 12 and 15 in the backseat. They were just laughing their heads off–all of them. I could not stop staring and actually said to myself, "What are they so happy about?" It was a sight I had never seen before and I was completely mesmerized. Now I know what they were so happy about.

Although my husband and I have laughed more together than we ever did before we met, we both would say we had never enjoyed such spontaneous laughter until we had children. We sit around the dinner table at least five nights a week, enjoying the conversation and the laughter.

John and I are constantly amazed at their developing wit. We want to raise our children in a home not only filled with love, but with laughter. We strive to do different activities the kids will think are fun, but we have discovered they really enjoy just being with us at home too.

One night I was cuddled on the bed with all four kids talking and laughing. I was asking questions like, "What color car do you want to have someday? Will your house be one story or two? How many children do you want to have?"

Then I posed the question, "Where is your favorite place in the world?" My ten-year-old son's answer warmed my heart. He said, "I like to go places, but I like to be home the best." Then my seven-year-old piped in with a "me too." I was expecting Disneyland or somewhere exciting but was thrilled to hear their true feelings.

It's my heart's desire to create a warm and fun environment they will love to be in. John and I often act very silly with the children and we tease them endlessly. We play hide and seek, we run through the house, we wrestle on the bed. And sometimes we push back the furniture and turn up loud music and dance. They love it. We love it.

Career stresses, paying bills, doing laundry and even rush hour traffic can make your nerves stand on edge. We mothers need to kick back and be goofy sometimes just as much as our children need us to.

And though we may not realize it, they need to *de-stress* too sometimes. My Grandma once said children's problems are just as big to them as ours are to us. My Grandma was a very wise woman. Their problems may be simply someone at school is no longer their friend, or they struggled on a math test, but it is a big problem in their little worlds.

Proverbs 17:22 says that a cheerful heart is good medicine. Laughing together often can help you over the humps and through the hard times. And it creates lasting memories your children will be telling their children about.

You are creating a legacy they will take into their own families someday. Push back the furniture and shake a leg. You will be the coolest mom ever.

Scripture: She is clothed with strength and dignity; she can laugh at the days to come. Proverbs 31:25

Challenge: I know your children make you smile every day. I challenge you to do something out of character tomorrow and watch your child's reaction. You both will giggle even if he or she thinks you have gone a little crazy. Continue to build on this and stay young at heart. Your cheerful heart will carry you throughout your daily duties.

# DAY 20

## A NEW CREATION

My wedding day was one of the best days of my life for so many reasons. First of all, I was marrying the man of my dreams, my absolute best friend. Our path to the altar had been long and messy. After walking down the aisle at the end of the ceremony, we slipped into a small classroom outside the sanctuary. We jumped up and down like we were five years old screaming, "We did it!" It was an amazing moment that I cherish dearly.

Another reason I loved my wedding day was because I was given a new name. I was taking on my husband's last name, so, in my mind, I was becoming a new person. In many ways I looked at it as a fresh start. It was as if I was getting do-over's for all my bad choices. With my new name, came a new beginning.

The truth is, though, we are already made new with Christ. A name change didn't change who I was, but Christ's blood did. Second Corinthians 5:17 says, "Therefore, if anyone is in Christ, he is a new creation; the old has gone, the new has come!" We are a renewed person after God's image and we have a renewed knowledge.

A concern I face in this stage of my life is what to share with my children when a question or subject arises about my younger years. In my selfish pride, I want to hide all of it from them. But then I genuinely want them to learn of God's grace and mercy and to know that their mother is a humble and thankful recipient of God's redemption.

While God protected me from many poor choices, He also allowed me to make mistakes when I was not seeking His will but looking to man for my self-worth. As a result of my mistakes, I have a deeper understanding of what God's grace truly means.

But for many years, I carried guilt with me. I knew God had forgiven me but I had a very hard time forgiving myself. The memories of my past would creep up and with them would come condemnation and embarrassment and shame. It took me many years to realize the devil was having a field day with me.

Romans 8:1 teaches there is no condemnation in those who are in Jesus Christ. But it was not my first tendency to hold fast to this word from God. The Bible also tells us in John 10:10 the enemy comes to kill, steal, and destroy and that he is the father of lies. I spent much too long letting the devil have a voice in my mind. The devil will lie to you and tell you if you are truly repentant for your sin, then you will feel guilty about it forever.

But 1 John 1:9 assures us that when we confess our sins to Him then He is faithful and just to forgive us. When Jesus disciplines me out of love, there is never guilt or condemnation with it, only conviction and love. My favorite part though, is the last part of this verse; he will "purify us from all unrighteousness." Not only will He forgive us, he will remove the guilt and destruction that sin can have on our lives. He will cleanse us so we can live holy lives. There is no disclaimer about your sin with this verse; it doesn't matter what our past looks like. We only have to confess our sin to Jesus. The devil will tell us whatever he can to keep us from living free with Jesus, but we know the truth. I hope no matter how messy your past is, you embrace this fact.

Don't let the lack of your own forgiveness of your mistakes keep you from living the abundant life Jesus intended for you. Face your future with the certainty that Jesus is with you every step of the way.

He believes in your abilities to parent your children. He chose you for the job, in spite of all your mistakes. Instead of hanging on to regret, celebrate His grace. You are a new creation and, may I say, a wonderful mother.

Scripture: Blessed are they whose transgressions are forgiven, whose sins are covered. Blessed is the man whose sin the Lord will never count against him. Romans 4:8-9

Challenge: Include in your prayer tonight, "Lord, please give me wisdom and discernment in raising my children. Help me to know the proper answers when they ask about my past or questions I am unsure how to answer. I thank You for Your grace and mercy and that You are just and faithful to forgive me. Please teach me how to forgive myself and to walk boldly with You."

# DAY 21

## FRUITFUL FINANCING

I thank God for a nerdy boyfriend my freshman year in college. He taught me about balancing a check book, because too frequently I would sit in my car at the ATM machine and wonder why it would not spit money out at me.

When I went to college I did not have a checking account of my own. One of my new friends told me to open one, so I marched to her bank and proudly sat in the cushy chair and filled out the information form. This same friend also helped me get my first credit card, but once it was maxed out to its $5000 limit, she did not tell me how to pay it off.

I learned nothing about finances while growing up, but I did learn about hard work. I quickly learned, however, that one without the other was futile.

I was in my second semester when my new boyfriend sat down with me in my dorm room and showed me how to reconcile my checking account. This became my monthly ritual, something I valued immediately. Because of this, I was very fortunate to have a balanced checkbook every month.

While I was a fast study in learning to reconcile my checkbook and keep the balance out of the red, it took me much too long to learn about the choke hold of debt. Credit card offers were a steady stream in my mailbox and I filled them out faithfully. After all, they were so generous to extend the offer. Department stores were the nicest because they would give me a 15% discount on the spot if I applied for their credit card.

I remember comparing the number of credit cards with my girlfriends my junior year in college. I had nine different credit cards, but one of my friends had twelve, so we thought she was the winner.

Years of experience have taught me no one with debt is a winner. Proverbs 22:7 says the borrower is servant to the lender. I found this to be so true. I was a slave to a mountain of debt and I didn't know where to start.

My belief system was that everyone had to have *some* debt, at least car payments and maybe even a small balance on a credit card or two. Through God's grace and guidance I have come to develop a different belief system.

My husband and I have learned the hard way how to better manage our money. We have made financial mistakes we both regret deeply, but it has taught us we do not have to be slave to anyone. We do not have to be in debt.

We drive older cars with high miles, but we have no car payment. We have no debt on credit cards, and our only debt is our mortgage. This was such a blessing to us during a period when my husband experienced a lay-off. Because we were not in great debt, we were able to maintain our lifestyle during this time and never had to miss or be late on a mortgage payment.

We also are committed to tithing every paycheck. We know with all of our hearts that God's math is much better than our math. When we are faithful to give God the first of our earnings, He is more than faithful to provide.

Looking back now, I know so many of my poor financial choices could have been avoided had I learned about money at an early age. Now I am committed to teaching my children to be good stewards of their finances. They do not have to repeat the same mistakes their father and I made.

When our oldest was barely five years old, I sat down with him and four quarters and showed him how to separate them into giving, saving and spending. We play board games that teach how to pay bills and spend money. And we talk at length about giving to others less fortunate.

While I am firmly against sharing the burden of financial struggles with children, I do strongly believe we can raise up a new generation of good stewards by teaching them how to handle money wisely.

Many call our world today a *microwave society* because we have to have what we want–now. Immediate gratification is prevalent among adults as well as children. This epidemic will greatly hurt our children's financial future if we are not educating them while they are still under our roof.

We have to teach them how to save and spend wisely. And most importantly, we have to teach them how to give.

Scripture: Honor the Lord with your wealth, with the firstfruits of all your crops; then your barns will be filled to overflowing, and your vats will brim over with new wine. Proverbs 3:9-10

Challenge: I believe it is never too early or too late to start teaching our children about finances. It all starts with a piggy bank at any age. Choose at least one age-appropriate lesson you can teach your child this week. Balancing numbers does not have to be your strength to be able to share what you know. You are doing such a great job already, Mom, and this is one area you do not want to leave out – unless you want them borrowing money from you when they are 40.

# DAY 22

## HEALTHY FRIENDSHIPS

When I was preparing for a speaking engagement centered on the subject of hope, I took the topic to my Bible study friends. I asked them what makes them lose hope, even though they are in a relationship with Christ.

I was thinking along the more shallow shores of not being able to lose the last ten pounds or allowing ourselves to be over-stressed and over-tired. I expected ongoing financial struggles or the stress of juggling family and career to be other answers. But these ladies' answers were deep and from real life. We finally narrowed our ideas to two leading hope stealers.

The first one was events or tragedies we can't explain: the sudden loss of a loved one, harmful events happening to our children, an affair or divorce, or a chronic or terminal illness.

The second was when someone we love or respect betrays us or lets us down. We had a thought-provoking conversation before we all came to the same conclusion—we simply do not have the answers as to why bad things happen. We also agreed we were so thankful to know the One who does.

While the first hope stealer is definitely worthy of discussion, I want to address when someone lets you down. While we are mothers with our whole hearts, we are also sisters, wives, and daughters with a great need for friends.

As mothers we constantly monitor our children's friends. We want to know the type of people they are being influenced by and if the influence is positive or negative. We see the importance of teaching our children to choose peers that are positive and encouraging, but sometimes we fail to take the same advice ourselves.

I know the hurt that stems from being betrayed by someone I thought was my friend and confidante. And I know that if you are over the age of five, you too have been betrayed by someone who hurt you deeply.

Along with a saddened heart, we are left with a decision to make. We have to choose to either forgive and move forward to a new positive relationship or to remain bitter and hurt.

Although it is hard to recognize, sometimes when a person leaves our life, it is a blessing. I once had a friend tell me I would fail when I started my own business. When I was selected as the National Young Mother of the Year, another friend told me I didn't know anything about motherhood because I did not have teenagers. I defended a childhood friend regarding a hateful note left on my car, only to find out it was indeed she who left it.

There are endless stories throughout my 40 plus years of times I have felt saddened and hurt by a friend's destructive words or betrayal of confidences. There are many reasons why one would betray a friend, but you cannot dwell on the answers to that. One of my close friends and I call that a *them problem* and not a *you problem.*

You have to take the same advice you give to your child – surround yourself with people who support you. It is often said you are the sum of your five closest friends. Keeping that in mind, are your closest friends encouragers? Do they love you with the love of Christ? Are they a blessing to those around them? Or do they tear people down to elevate themselves? Do they gossip and complain all the time?

We all are continually growing and maturing in our respective walks with God. We need friends who support that growth and who walk on the path beside us. Our daily goal should be to strive to be more Christ-like. And never forget, He is a friend who will never let us down, never betray us and never leave us alone.

If you have been hurt by someone, and it has kept you from developing healthy relationships today, it is time to take that wound to Jesus. After all, He knows better than anyone what it is like to be betrayed by a close friend.

He understands and not only will He give you healing, He will bring the right relationships into your life. He is so trustworthy with all areas of our lives, and that includes our friendships. We need each other because life can sometimes be messy and hard.

Surround yourself with those who will link arms with you on this rollercoaster ride. And just as we teach our children, let's all walk through our days practicing the Golden Rule: Do to others what you would have them do to you.

Scripture: Greater love has no one than this, that he lay down his life for his friends. John 15:13

Challenge: Be honest in admitting to yourself if you have allowed a past hurt to keep you from developing healthy friendships with other women. Pray over your closest friends and ask God to give you wisdom and discernment regarding these close relationships. If you are blessed with a supportive and loyal friend, tell her how much you appreciate her character and integrity. Tell her how thankful you are she is a part of your life.

# Day 23

## The Right Counsel

Until about five years ago, my mom and I had frequent disagreements about her hairstyle and her hairstylist. I am happy to report she has finally come around.

While the rest of the world had long since let go of curly permanents, my mom still loved them. While the rest of us had graduated into highlights, Mom's hairstylist was still *frosting* her hair. This hairstylist continued to damage Mom's hair but no amount of begging could convince her to change stylists.

One day on the phone, Mom told me my stepdad wanted her to get a permanent because he liked the style. As I pleaded with her that it was the 2000's and not 1985, she again stated her husband liked it.

My stepdad is in law enforcement and likes to wear his hair in a military style *high and tight,* leaving him almost hairless. Finally I cried out, "Mom, you are taking hair advice from a bald man. Never take hair advice from a bald man!" We both erupted into laughter, but I had just invented a new motto for life.

I don't know which we women are better at, asking our friends for advice or giving it, solicited or not. Because mothers have so many balls they juggle between home and career, it is a common occurrence for us to run into a hurdle that causes stress. As a result we like to know what others in our situation would do. . . or we are looking for someone to validate a decision we are making.

I have found too many different opinions can cause confusion in our minds and we end up feeling less certain than we did in the beginning. The greater danger comes when we continue asking others for advice, even though it is contrary to what God wants us to do.

I have been guilty of taking a problem to my friends before I even think to pray about it. Jesus should always be our first step in seeking guidance, but it has not always been my initial tendency. As I continue to work on this area of my life, I have also learned to be more selective with those I seek advice from.

That is where my new motto struck a chord with me. If a mother has unruly children who disrespect her and others, I do not go to her when I am facing a behavior problem. When my husband and I want to learn more about being good stewards of our money, we do not seek out someone who is deep in debt and living paycheck to paycheck.

In every area of my life I want to be mentored by someone I respect in whatever area I need to grow and be guided in. When it comes to my family and parenting, I am very careful who I let influence me. Although there are many great parenting books on the market today, there are many more poor parenting books written by authors who do not share my values and moral beliefs. As a result, I do not own a lot of parenting books. I feel like I know my children better than anyone in the world, just as you know your children the best.

I love to glean parenting ideas and tips from books and other mothers, but before I implement them, I want to be sure they will not be harmful to my child's nature. Although my four children came from the same gene pool, each one is so different from the others. So it is safe to say what will work for one child will be completely useless for another. I am a big advocate of reading and learning from books, but if I am going to read on a topic I want to grow in, I make sure the author does not contradict what the Bible teaches.

One of my biggest concerns for women in our society today is who is influencing us daily, especially through the media. There is a very popular television talk-show host who has had incredible influence for more than two decades. And while she is neither married nor a mother, she frequently gives advice to millions on these two topics. She also promotes being spiritual and believing in a *higher power* no matter what *your god looks like.*

Those who give these kinds of opinions and philosophies are very dangerous because the message is packaged in a subtle and sometimes humorous delivery. Proverbs 4:23 says, "Above all else, guard your heart, for it is the wellspring of life."

If we are not carefully guarding our hearts and our minds, we can be seduced by people who are not qualified to give us counsel and can who pull us from God's word. It is very important for us as mothers to be alert to who and what is influencing us, because we are the main influencers on our children.

While I believe it is biblical and responsible to allow ourselves to be mentored by the right people, I am still learning to seek Jesus first and foremost. I know I will make mistakes along the way, but I am practicing listening for God's voice. I want it to be louder than any other voice I hear.

And I am committed to avoiding all bald men with bad hair advice.

Scripture: The plans of the righteous are just, but the advice of the wicked is deceitful. Proverbs 12:5

Challenge: Take a moment to ponder what your first reaction is when you have an obstacle or stressful decision to make. Do you take it to Jesus first or to friends? Think about whether you seek advice from those who have proven themselves knowledgeable or successful in the area you are struggling in. More importantly, do they encourage godly principles in helping you make a tough decision? If there are things you feel need changing and you are seeking mentorship, take your concern to God first.

# Day 24

## The Value in Chatting

My husband and I love to talk to each other. It has been like that from the first time we sat down together after work one night. Before we knew it, two hours had passed in what seemed like 10 minutes.

While we were in college we would frequent an all-night breakfast joint filled with college kids. More than one occasion led to us watching the sun come up because we were so absorbed in conversation. So I guess it is no surprise that we produced four little talkers.

We have very lively dinners that consist of loud volume and talking over each other to tell our own stories. We are still learning to use an *inside voice* and *wait patiently for our turn to talk*.

I remember when we had our first official family meeting—it was quite an event. We had three little wiggly boys anxious for their turn to talk and a bright-eyed two-year-old girl just watching everything the boys did and trying to imitate them.

We created a list of rules for our household and let them choose the punishments for breaking those rules. They loved having input. They felt valued because they knew their opinions mattered.

We don't have weekly family meetings, but we do have them on a regular basis as needed, and they get so excited when it is time to have one. One of the older boys will post a sign in the kitchen with the time and place the meeting is to be held. When it's not family meeting time, sometimes we just pile on our bed and I ask them all types of silly questions. *What kind of car do you want to drive when you grow up? How many kids will you* have? *What will their names be? Where do you want to vacation to?* We take turns answering the questions, and it is so fun to hear their individuality shine through and the great plans they have for themselves.

Friday nights became a weekly tradition in our family when our oldest was five years old. We labeled it *camp out* night and we all put on our pajamas, watch a movie, eat popcorn and ice cream, and stay up past bedtime. It has come to be a big deal in our family and several days before, the conversation centers around which movie we are going to rent. This tradition gives us something to talk about and plan together.

I have begun to feel more peaceful that we are setting a good foundation for open communication with our children. It is my heart's desire they will always feel comfortable coming to me with anything they want to talk about, whether it be a joyous topic or a hard subject they don't know how to handle.

I am inquisitive with them, and as they grow older I ask even more questions. When it is appropriate, I will give them reasons for why I told them to do something or didn't allow something else. I believe communication is a two-way street, and I have to be the leader in teaching them how valuable it is to a relationship, starting with the relationship with their family.

Anytime we spend communicating, we are benefiting from sacred quality time. I know quality time is something all mothers ponder on, worry about, and strive to have more of. It is hard balancing a family and a career, and I know as a mom you can feel pulled in several different directions.

Working from home, I have felt guilty countless times for shooing a child away when I was on the phone with a client. Mothers of multiple children can relate to my fears of not wanting one to get lost in the mix because he isn't as vocal as another. Every day is a test to stay sensitive to each one and his individual needs.

Let me assure you that you are doing the best job you can do. We will miss the mark sometimes, but each day is a new opportunity to be a little better. Communication is an important key to keeping our families strong and close-knit, as well as less vulnerable to outside influences that may not be so positive.

You are a great influence, Mom, and your children are only going to benefit from time spent chatting with you.

Scripture: My sheep listen to my voice; I know them, and they follow me. John 10:27

Challenge: Three of the scariest but most fun questions I ever asked my children were these: What do you like about me? What do I do that you really like? What would you like for me to do better? I challenge you to take a deep breath and ask these questions. I think you will love the answers. And you will grow from them too.

# Day 25

## The Greatest Book

As I stated in my introduction, I love to read. I am such a book junkie that we are bursting at the seams on every bookshelf we have—not to mention the boxes filled with books in the garage.

I love to buy books; I love the look of a beautiful hardback on my shelf and the feel of a good paperback in my hands. The gift of the Kindle slowed down my purchase of hard copy books somewhat, but didn't slow down my reading. To add more to the mess, my husband also is an avid reader. He always has a book going and three more waiting in the wings.

I have been told many times that a person is the sum of the books they read and the people they associate with. I am convinced this is solid truth. There is so much to be learned from books, even fiction, and as much as I love movies, I think books are the best movies because they play in my imagination.

The love of reading is one thing I hope and pray my children pick up from their father and me. I have said many times that while I won't pay them to do chores, I will pay them to read a book and give me a report about it. There is so much value in reading, especially when we are feeding our minds with the right material.

I talk about the importance of reading with my children consistently. And while they have not developed my affinity for it yet, I am still holding out hope.

I have found reading is a great way to share quality time with them. The littlest ones I will read to, and as they begin to read I have them read stories to me. My ten-year-old son has always been an advanced reader and last year he and I began reading classic books together.

We started with *Tom Sawyer* and read a chapter at bedtime. We both looked forward to what was going to happen next and couldn't wait to get back into it. Currently we are reading *The Wind in the Willows* and are also searching for our next written adventure.

The most important lesson I hope they can learn from me is the value of reading the greatest book of all time. The Bible contains the greatest history lessons, great battles, beautiful love stories, examples of loyal friendships and excellent leaders. On and on the education goes.

The amazing thing to me is although it is more than 2000 years old, it is still relevant to everything going on in my life today. There is nothing I need guidance on that I cannot turn the pages of God's word and find an answer.

One of the ways God speaks to us is through His word. If I am not staying plugged into reading my Bible, I am missing opportunities for Him to speak to me. I want my children to learn this and build on it for the rest of their lives.

Last year I started doing my Bible study with them at the table while they are doing their homework. Not only am I right there to help them, but they see the importance I am placing on studying God's word. It is not always the easiest way to concentrate for me and I do find myself being interrupted more than I would like, but I am hopeful the sacrifice of a quiet study time will plant a seed that will grow like crazy in their little hearts.

Nurturing their spiritual walks is far too important for me to give up any opportunity to be an example and teach them the value of reading the Bible. And as we know, the best way to teach is to show.

So I am continuing on with my reading campaigns and taking their groans in stride as they are learning. It definitely has not been a cake-walk getting them to read every night, but it will be worth the fights when they finally come over to my side.

Scripture: All scripture is God-breathed and is useful for teaching, rebuking, correcting and training in righteousness, so that the man of God may be thoroughly equipped for every good work. 2 Timothy 3:16-17

Challenge: No matter the age of your child, I challenge you to read with them for a small amount of time each night. If he is a teenager it will be a great bonding time, even if he thinks you are a little crazy at first. And take any opportunity to read your Bible with your child or at least start by letting him see you study God's word. Your emphasis on it will make them take note of it for themselves.

# DAY 26

## ENCOURAGING WORDS

Our team was down by three runs, it was the bottom of the ninth with two outs and two people on base. Of course, as fate would have it, I was up to bat.

I didn't even like softball; I only played because I liked sports and liked being part of a team. I was not a great player; I only made the roster so there were enough players to make a team. Batting was my weakest area because I was too timid to do it well.

Although it was many, many years ago, I still remember walking up to bat feeling scared to death. As I walked up to the plate, I heard a teammate ask who was up to bat.

I heard someone else say my name and then I heard her say, "I'm going to start packing up the gear. The game is over." She had zero faith or belief I could hit the ball. This girl used words to defeat and harm others.

Another teammate said, "No. Don't start packing up." Then she began clapping and cheering for me. This girl used her words for encouragement and support.

I took my position staring at the pitcher and prayed for her to throw four balls. I stood frozen while the pitcher threw three strikes in a row. I could hear the second girl still clapping and cheering with encouragement at every pitch, but the first girl's words had already left their mark. Three strikes flew past me and I never swung the bat even once.

While that moment was humiliating, it has served me well because there were several lessons to be learned that day. One of the most obvious lessons that has helped me achieve success in many areas is I will always *swing* at my goals. I may miss, I may strike out, but I will go down swinging, nonetheless.

The more important lesson I learned is I never want to be that first girl. I don't want to be the person who uses her words to bring people discouragement or hurt. I don't want to be the negative voice to my family, my friends, my husband, and especially my children.

I believe in my children as I know you believe in yours and all of their God-given qualities. Daily I make sure to use my words to encourage and uplift my children. I want to build their confidence and their self-esteem. I will tell them God made them so special, and they are going to do great things in their lives.

Although they change almost daily, I talk to them about their dreams and assure them they can do whatever they want to do. I make it a point to shower them with praise constantly.

But the number of times I have said something hurtful to them either unknowingly or out of anger makes my heart break. It only takes one time to say something that can break their spirits or tear at their fragile confidence. Words are so powerful.

The Bible is full of illustrations teaching us how our words can have lasting impact on someone's life or our own life. Careless speech and out of control words can cause us to sin and affect our relationship with others and more importantly, with God.

While our children are under our roof, they are heavily influenced by the words they hear come out of our mouths. Especially the words directed at them.

With the four individual personalities I am raising, I have to be careful with each one, as one may be more sensitive to something than another. My husband and I have a playful relationship and we tease each other endlessly. This playfulness carries over into our relationship with our children.

Our oldest son loves this playfulness and we can tease back and forth with him. Our second son is more literal. While he has a smart wit, he also is very sensitive to certain types of teasing. We have to be careful with what we say to all of them even in joking.

My children also learn the power of words when they hear my conversations with other people. If they hear me talking to a friend and complimenting her or telling her she is a great mom or an excellent teacher, they learn to speak words of encouragement to others. If they hear me gossiping about someone or complaining about a friend or family member, they learn to be judgmental and negative towards others.

I want them to be like the second girl from my softball team. I want them to learn to use God's love to share encouragement and hope with others in their everyday lives.

It is very hard to watch what I say every minute of every day. Some days it feels like I am fighting a losing battle with controlling my tongue. I know I have no chance of being able to control my words without God's help every day.

I am very certain you also encourage your children with belief, faith, and praise. Every day you are striving to be a positive influence to him or her, and you are building a strong foundation that will serve them the rest of their lives.

Like me, I am sure there are times you miss the mark and feel guilty and regretful. We both are in need of God's guidance and grace every minute. Let's commit together to continue positive speaking to our children.

This is one goal I know I am not giving up on. No matter what, I will keep swinging.

Scripture: He who guards his lips guards his life, but he who speaks rashly will come to ruin. Proverbs 13:3

Challenge: Every morning for the next week, commit to starting the day showering your child with praise and encouragement. Then to continue building this habit of speaking positive words, speak words of encouragement to someone–a friend or coworker or family member–for the next week. Not only will you bless others, you will find yourself being blessed with God's presence and encouragement as well.

# DAY 27

## LEGACY

Legacy is a word that conjures up a myriad of emotions in me. The first emotion is anxiety because it makes me think of dying. A legacy is something you leave behind or what you are remembered for long after you are gone.

And I do think about what I want my children to remember about me, but not just when I am dancing in heaven. I think of what I want them to remember from their childhood when they are adults.

My husband and I have lain in bed at night and joked about what we say about our parents and speculate about what our kids may say about us someday with their spouses. But it is also a subject I take seriously and try to use as a guide in how I manage my time.

I know if I were to ask you for the positives you want your children to remember about you, the list would be as endless as mine. But I also know there are a few things that make the top of the list—the *biggies* I like to call them.

When I sharpened my ideas of what I wanted my children to take hold of while they are under my roof, I realigned my priorities. As a result I also gained a sense of peace about my schedule.

At the top of my list I want them to remember I had a deep relationship with Christ. By no means is it perfect, and I know more than anyone there is still much growth needed. But I want them to know deep in their hearts my first love was God. I want them to have learned by watching me that

Christ is Someone they can not only talk to as a Best Friend, but One they can cry with and laugh with.

I want them to see me serve and care for others during difficult times because of the love of Christ. Many times growing up, I went with my grandma, May Belle, to visit an elderly shut-in. We baked many treats to take to someone as an act of kindness and we physically went to check on friends who had been sick. Grandma never talked about why we were doing it, but I learned from her actions.

Another item at the top of my list is a heart of gratitude. This one drives my children crazy sometimes, I know, because their eyes glaze over a little when I start harping on it. My children are growing up in the age of electronics and advanced technology. We have so many comforts and luxuries they can't even begin to fully understand how spoiled we are.

They can't wrap their minds around how Mom had to move off her chair to turn the dial on the television to change the channel. My husband and I both are always telling them how blessed we are to have a nice home, plenty of food to eat, many clothes in our closets, and all the extras we enjoy that we don't need but want.

I realize it is hard for them to understand that not everyone in the world lives like we do. They are still young and their world is very small. But I take opportunities when I can to share with others what God has blessed us with. When I do this, I involve the children as much as possible.

I know every good thing I have has come from God and I am so grateful and humbled by all He has given me – not just material things, but my husband and children He has given me. Most importantly, God has given me the blessings of His presence in my life. I want my children to know my gratitude to God for all these blessings.

Another legacy I want my children to have is a healthy balance of hard work and play. It wasn't until I was a working adult with a child of my own did I realize this was one of the legacies Grandma left for me.

Grandma would work hard to maintain her little farm and garden, work inside the house with the duties, and then she would spend hours playing with me. Even when I was a teenager we would make up games outside to play together. We would go for bike rides and long walks. Sometimes we would go to the lake.

She worked when it was time to work, but when there was an important event in my life or even something minor like a ball game, she would stop working to be there to support me. I try to implement that same parenting style in my home today.

I want my children to learn a strong work ethic and the pride of a job done well. But I want them to remember the activities we do as a family that create a sense of balance. Everything from our short evening walks to camping trips to silly games in the house count as our play time. I want them to see the value of working hard but also know they are my first priority.

One mother's list is no better or worse than another's. It just will be different based on our own beliefs or upbringing. But it is important for us to all know what kind of legacy we want to leave our children. It will free us up to concentrate on the things of real value to us and spend less time worrying about the ones not as important.

Whether you have ever thought about it or not, you are building a legacy. And I would bet it is an amazing one.

Scripture: Follow my example, as I follow the example of Christ. 1 Corinthians 11:1

Challenge: Ask your children what they will remember about you when they are grown up with families of their own. The answers will likely surprise you, and be fun to hear. I had one say he will remember I made good dinners and one who said I was funny. I can live with that.

# Day 28

## To Your Good Health

Okay, don't hate me. But you knew we had to talk about it sometime. Let's get physical, physical. Or at least healthy.

For those of you already doing triathlons, you have my permission to go ahead and enjoy sweet dreams. This is for the rest of us who are grumbling under our breath at moms like you. With love, of course.

Our health is our most precious commodity. All the money or fame in the world cannot measure up to our good health. We deserve it and our children deserve it. I am not talking about a number on the scale or a single digit on your pants tag, but about a healthy body best able to serve you and your family.

Growing up, I was very athletic and trim and stayed like that until I hit about 28 years old. Then after pregnancy complications and multiple miscarriages, I gradually stopped exercising. Before I knew it, I was almost 37 years old, had 4 babies and 20 extra pounds. And I absolutely hated looking in the mirror. But more crucial, I was no longer healthy.

Chasing toddlers around the house logged more miles than when I was on a track team. Not to mention carrying a 20 pound little person on my hip all day should have been better than lifting weights at a gym. So why did I feel so poorly and have such little energy?

Over the next couple of years my health declined a little more and I could not lose a pound no matter how much I starved. But, although I cooked a healthy dinner every night, the rest of my diet consisted of foods high in sugar and preservatives. For the first time in my life, I craved sweets to the point of not being able to control myself.

The highly processed foods and junk food tasted good for sure, but the effects they were having on my blood sugar and heart were not benefiting me at all. My energy level was at an all time low, but I just blamed it on the demands of having four young children. I finally came to the point I wanted to be healthy for my children's sake.

I was witnessing friends my age struggle with obesity, have heart attacks, or take medication for high blood pressure and diabetes. It scared me into taking action. Being sick and tired of being sick and tired led me on a journey to educate myself in how to achieve better health for myself, without the use of prescription medications.

After researching the internet, reading several books, and talking to holistic practitioners, I finally learned how to treat my body. I found one book in particular that gave me great success. It taught me more about my body type and what is best for me individually.

The first few weeks were miserable—I don't mind telling you. But I knew I was doing something to not only benefit me for the rest of my life, but my children as well. What I was doing was not a diet but a lifestyle change. My intentions were, and still are, to live like this the rest of my life.

The steps I took may not be what you need to do, but they were what I had to do to start on my path to a healthier lifestyle. I began by cutting out all sugars and I substituted honey, agave or stevia when needed. Then I began eating foods I didn't like such as kale, carrots, celery, and many other vegetables I thought were evil. I still would rather eat a potato chip, but it is about eating to live and not living to eat.

While many give up eating meat when choosing a healthier diet, this is not an option for me. So I learned to cut back my portions to a smaller amount and eat more vegetables. All of these changes were met with great complaining and murmuring under my breath. Yes, I was taking the steps …but I didn't have to like it.

Then I began to drag my flabby, fluffy, tired body on walks. Slowly I added more distance and then speed. Jogging is not for everyone but walking can be. After a while I began to find experience the old me that enjoyed exercising and had more energy than I had had in years.

Finding a plan I could learn a great deal from has benefited me and my whole family. We all snack on fruit, use less than half the sugar than before and enjoy our *cheat treats* when we have them. We drink a lot of water and my children are only allowed to have one weekly soda on Friday nights. Our pediatrician loves me.

I had begun to really worry about how my children's healthy habits would develop as fast food and frozen meals became more prevalent in our society. It is common knowledge our nation's obesity rate is increasing dramatically. Because of this, our children are at great risk to suffer from diseases caused by obesity and unhealthy lifestyles. The realization for me was healthy habits for my children have to start with me.

I know just like me, you do not want your children to have anything but excellent health and a long, energetic life. And I want you to have excellent health and a long, energetic life to enjoy with them. The time you invest in your health is one of the best investments you can make.

If you find there are some changes you need to make in your health, be encouraged that you can do it. You can do all things through Christ who gives you strength. It won't be easy at first but it will be worth it.

And I know from experience you will feel a great sense of pride in yourself you have not had in a long time. God has great plans for your life and He needs you to be healthy so you can enjoy all that He has for you.

Scripture: Dear friend, I pray that you may enjoy good health and that all may go well with you, even as your soul is getting along well. 3 John 2

Challenge: Whether you need to only make a couple of small changes or many big ones, start small. Trying to take on too many changes at once will only lead to failure. Consider getting a full physical before you start. This will give you a base line on your health numbers to compare as you go along. Find a good book or someone knowledgeable to teach you better diet and exercise options right for you. And tomorrow, go for a walk with your children. They will love it–and so will you.

# Day 29

## Stepping Out of Regret

Oh, how regret can be such an ugly thing. It can take on a life of its own and rear its ugly head anytime you start to have a moment's peace. I don't think any of us are without regret of some sort.

Everyone has something in her past she wishes she had done differently. We all have those *skeletons in the closet*—only some are bigger than others. I have often joked that if you were to open my proverbial closet, a big ole bone would clonk you on the head.

Those of us with a messy path behind us are intimately familiar with regret. And we are the same ones, I hope, who are intimately familiar with God's grace and mercy. Most of the time regret is birthed out of things we wished we had *not* done. I have more of those than I dare try to count.

But what I want to talk with you about is not the regret of mistakes we have made, but the regret of things we never attempted. Opportunities we did not seize, most likely out of fear. Maybe it was a fear of failure, fear of what others may think, or even fear of responsibility if we succeeded.

Each year my children's school has a different motto for the school year. This year the theme is, "Do It Afraid" based on 2 Timothy 1:7 KJV. It says "For God hath not given us the spirit of fear; but of power, and of love, and of a sound mind." I believe this is a verse we all should commit to memory so we can call on it when we are facing an opportunity but are fearful to move forward.

I once made a magnet for my refrigerator that said, *When we look back on our lives, we will regret the things we didn't do more than the things we did.* I recognized there had been many things in my life I had wanted to do but didn't have the courage to step out and try. As hard as it is still, I am now trying to not let an opportunity pass me by that I will regret later on not having attempted.

Being the nerd I am, I once made a list of all the things I would regret not having done before I was 40 years old. My list included everything from spending time with my children to running a marathon to publishing books. Some items on my list were about my family, some were just about me and my personal growth. I didn't cross everything off before the age of 40, but I am still working on that list.

Sometime later, *bucket lists* became popular because of a hit movie, so I keep expanding my list. Many items on my list are scary for me, as I am sure yours are too. But neither one of us can let fear become such a loud voice that it drowns out the voice of God.

There are likely things on your list that can bring glory to God when you step out in faith and do them. These are opportunities to grow our faith and draw closer to Him. The devil will do what he can to keep us locked in a place of fear. He will do anything he can to keep us from bringing God glory.

We cannot make the mistake of thinking the devil is passive and has no interest in our lives. And when the devil knows our weak area, he will pitch a tent there until we call on God's power to overcome it. According to Romans 8:37, "...we are more than conquerors through him who loved us."

We have everything we need through Christ to step out of our comfort zone and *do it afraid.* Whether you are paralyzed with regret from a past full of things you wished you had not done or opportunities you did not take advantage of, you have to forgive yourself. Jesus has long since forgiven you, now you must forgive yourself and more forward.

Once I asked my Grandma if she would change her past if she could and her answer was that she would not. She said that sure, there were things she wished she had done differently, but a person cannot live a life with regret. You can only look forward and live your life. That simple advice helped me to glance backwards only to learn from my mistakes, and to focus on what God has laid before me.

For the remainder of my life, I want to have fewer regrets than I have in my current past. In order to do that, I am going to have to step out in faith and attempt to do things I am afraid to do. I would guess you have a few things you need to look for outside your comfort zone, as well.

If your child was fearful of stepping out in faith, I know you would encourage him with wisdom and prayer. You would explain to him the accomplishments that he can achieve just by trying. You would share how God can receive great glory when one of His children does something in His name and His strength. And I am sure you would include that part of growing at any age is trying new things and stretching ourselves.

The obvious question is, will you follow your own wise advice? I am encouraging you and I will be praying for you. In fact, let's pray for each other.

Scripture: For you did not receive a spirit that makes you a slave again to fear, but you received the Spirit of sonship. Romans 8:15

Challenge: If you have not already done so, I challenge you to make your own bucket list. Don't be conservative when making this list, be bold. Write down things that scare you, items you would want to attempt if you knew there was no way you could fail. Pray over your list and then choose one that you can start on immediately. Let your child know what you are doing. He or she will be so proud and will be your biggest cheerleader. You are already Supermom to them.

# Day 30

## Honor the Sabbath

Do you know how you can read the same passage in the Bible several times but then one time that same verse jumps off the page at you? Or a topic stands out when you're reading one book of the Bible, and then you find almost the same words in another book of the Bible?

I know God is trying to tell me something when that happens to me. I have always gone to church on Sundays and considered it the Lord's day. But over the years as more children came along and with it more work to be done, Sundays evolved into a catch-up day to complete unfinished tasks. This became just a way of life for us and not something I put much thought into.

I had been praying for God to teach me how to have balance in my life and how to demonstrate it for my children. I believe He has answered my prayer by bringing certain scriptures to light for me. First, I came across Isaiah 58:13-14 that talks about keeping the Lord's Day holy and honorable and as a result we will find our joy in the Lord. It teaches us that God has designed one day to be set aside to stop our normal daily activities to rest physically and be renewed spiritually and mentally. Being obedient to this will allow us to grow in our joy and delight in the Lord.

Then I came across Jeremiah 17:22 *by accident* and found God telling us not to do any work on the Sabbath but to keep it holy.

I learned in Sunday School as a child that God created the heavens and the earth in six days and on the seventh day he rested from all his work.

So while this is something I have known all of my life, I don't think I fully understood the significance of this until recently.

I also have known my entire life that one of the Ten Commandments is to keep the Sabbath day holy. But again, I am not sure I knew how to apply this to my life. Going to church on Sundays is only part of what God intended the Sabbath day for.

As I read more about honoring the Sabbath day, I began to see how obeying God's command will keep me from being overwhelmed and fatigued. If I will observe the Lord's Day the way God meant for me to, then my mind will have a break from the stresses of everyday life and busyness. I can then focus on God's word and spend time in fellowship with Him.

I will grow spiritually and benefit from the peace and strength I can only gain from Him. Equally as important, I will have physical rest from the previous six days of working hard. This is going to contribute to better overall health as well, because I am not pushing my body to the point of exhaustion.

God created this day to be a source of blessing for us from the very beginning. Genesis 2:3 says God blessed the seventh day and made it holy. These passages are not telling us that in order to be obedient we are to sit all day reading the Bible and praying. But we are to lay aside our work for the day and avoid activities which distract us from the purpose of the day. The Sabbath is providing us one day a week to escape the concerns of the world and enjoy fellowship with Him.

I realize some people do shift work or a similar career and have no choice but to work on Sundays. But I believe it is important to still observe one day just to meditate and fellowship with Him, as we rest and renew our spirits.

I am disappointed it has taken me so long into adulthood to understand the significance of the Sabbath and what a blessing God has given us with this commandment. But I am so grateful He has been teaching me this over the past few weeks and speaking to me through His word.

Although it is tempting to get caught up with unfinished work on Sundays, I am committed to being obedient to God's command. Not only will I grow closer to Him, I will enjoy my family time as we honor the Sabbath together.

I am thankful I can teach my children at an early age what took me many years to learn. And I am also grateful I will be rested and rejuvenated to start my week. I will have more balance in my life, which is an answer to my prayer.

I felt it was important to share with you what I have learned. If you have been feeling fatigued to the point of exhaustion and your mind feels like it never rests, then this is a vital lesson for you too. There is freedom and renewal in being obedient to His commandments. And let's be honest, Mom, we both need that.

Scripture: Remember the Sabbath day by keeping it holy. Six days you shall labor and do all your work, but the seventh day is a Sabbath to the Lord your God. Exodus 20: 8-10a

Challenge: In trying to learn more about the Sabbath, I found there are so many places throughout both the Old and New Testament teaching about this very thing. There is still so much I have to learn. I challenge you to study with me starting with Matthew 12:1-13. More importantly, I challenge you to start this week observing the Sabbath by honoring Him and not working on unfinished chores. I am anxious for you to experience the sense of rejuvenation and peace that I know you will find from your obedience.

# DAY 31

## JESUS IS THE ONLY WAY

A while back I visited with some moms at a friend's party. This was the first time I had met these ladies and I enjoyed chatting with them about their families.

One mother made a statement that has haunted me since the party. She said she didn't want to teach her children about God but wanted to let them explore all religions for themselves when they are older. I sat in silence as my heart broke for her and her children.

In the crowd of ladies talking, I don't know what would have been appropriate for me to say. Even today I still don't know what I should have said, I just hate that I didn't say anything.

There is nothing I want in my life more than to raise my children to have a personal relationship with Jesus Christ. Ultimately, it will be their choice. But while they are under my watch, I feel it is my responsibility to teach them all I can about God. This is a responsibility I do not take lightly.

As a Christian mother, I have to be the voice for teaching them about God in a world that is becoming louder in its promotion of new age spirituality and atheism. The foundation I am providing for them today is what will help carry them into a strong faith in God as adults. If I leave it up to the world to teach them about God, I am leaving their salvation and the eternal consequences in unreliable hands.

The Bible clearly tells us believing in Jesus Christ is the only way to get to heaven. John 14:6 says, "Jesus answered, 'I am the way and the truth and the life. No one comes to the Father except through me.'" In addition to teaching my children what the Truth is, I also have to prepare them for what they may face from others outside our home or church.

There are many people in society who believe they will go to heaven simply because they are a good person. Others believe there is no heaven or hell. What I am finding more prevalent today is that many believe they don't have to believe in the one true God, but only a higher power.

As Christians today, we can be challenged that faith in God is only for those who are too weak to exist in this world. Others ask how Christians can be so arrogant to believe the Bible is the real and only truth.

I believe there are ways to teach and prepare my children with age-appropriate language and timing. I also educate them about other religious beliefs and denominations. While I want to help build a strong faith in Jesus Christ, I also want to teach them to not be disrespectful of others, but to be an example. Challenging someone else's belief is not the best way to lead someone to Jesus, but living out our faith with words and actions will be much more valuable.

My prayer for myself over the years has been to be bolder in sharing the plan of salvation with unbelievers. My heart is heavy from missed opportunities of witnessing to others because I was too timid to speak up. This is an area I will continue to pray over and grow in with God's help.

Jesus commissioned us in Matthew 28:19 to share the gospel with all people in all nations, and our home is our first mission field. If you are a new Christian and have not yet had the opportunity to teach your child about Jesus, don't be discouraged. Rather, relish the fact that all of heaven is celebrating over your salvation. The Bible says in Luke 15:7 that there will be more rejoicing in heaven over one sinner who repents.

Now that you are enjoying fellowship with Jesus, you can rely on Him to give you wisdom and guidance in sharing your faith with your child, no matter his age. Teaching our children about a true and real relationship with Jesus is not a one-time conversation but something they will learn over time.

My heart's desire for you, Mom, is to know Christ intimately first. Because until you know Him, you will never fully grasp how precious you are. I believe when you are walking in His Light, you are going to raise up godly men and women who will impact the world in an amazing way.

Scripture: Train a child in the way he should go, and when he is old he will not turn from it. Proverbs 22:6

Challenge: I challenge you to visit your local Christian bookstore as soon as possible. There you will find age-appropriate books, babies to young adults, to aid you in teaching your child God's Word. No matter the age of your child, find a book you can read together and discuss what you have read. This is a good place to start in teaching your child that there is only one true God and there is only one way into heaven: through Jesus Christ our Savior. I encourage you to enlist in a weekly church service or youth group for your child if you are not already involved. It will be an instrumental tool you both can benefit from.